If You Plant It, They Will Come
The Story Of How We Started Our Butterfly Garden...
...and Other Bits of Information

by Cynthia Harrington

© 2012 Cynthia Harrington is this book's author. The book author retains sole copyright to his or her contributions to this book.

Unless otherwise designated, all text, and photographs in this book are the copyrighted material of Cynthia Harrington, or other contributors who are given credit, and are not to be used in any way without explicit permission. Please respect national and international copyright laws.

All photographs in this book were taken by Vince DeMattia, unless otherwise indicated.

If You Plant It, They Will Come

Food for Thought!

Happiness can be as elusive as a
fluttering butterfly, But as easily
attainable as a crawling caterpillar

~Brian G. Jett

The Butterfly Whisperer!

"Happiness is like a butterfly which, when pursued, is always beyond our grasp, but, if you will sit down quietly, may alight upon you."

Nathaniel Hawthorne

This book is dedicated to my Mother and Father; Myriall and Walt, my Brothers and Sister; Tom, Skip, Donald and Marion and lastly to my Darling Vince, without whom this book would never have been written.

Vince encouraged me to write about my project and he was quick to rush me to the nursery to buy plants when I needed more food for the caterpillars. He bought dirt and pots so I could keep the project going and he was always ready with his camera; providing the lion's share of the photographs. Because of his willingness to be there every step of the way, I was able to bring this project to fruition and release generations of new butterflies. I now have a legacy I can pass on to my family.

When I was a child, I always remembered my Dad reading and writing. He was an avid reader and taught all his children to respect books and embrace the knowledge that could be learned from them. It seemed as though he was always writing something; articles, poems, short stories and books. Back in his day, it was difficult to get a book published and I remember him submitting several manuscripts, but alas, nothing ever became of them. Now that he is no longer with us, it seemed only fitting that I should write a book about one of my passions and publish it.

I never really thought of writing a book before, but I have spent over two years on this project and now that the house is up for sale, it may be coming to an end. My experience is something I treasure because I don't know of anyone else that has taken the "next step" after planting a butterfly garden of nectar plants to attract butterflies. I have been raising butterflies from eggs and releasing them. As of this writing, we have released a total of 559 butterflies and still counting. This total includes; Monarch, Swallowtail, Sulphur and now Gulf Fritillary butterflies.

We started from scratch and had to learn everything from books, articles and the internet. Once I started collecting eggs, I kept notes and these writings are from my own personal experiences as well as what information I gleaned along the way.

***My hope is that I will encourage others to increase the butterfly population in their own neighborhoods. It only takes one plant to get started.**

If You Plant It, They Will Come

Welcome to Cynthia's Butterfly Garden...and sanctuary, created at our home in Florida.

This butterfly sanctuary is a 110 square foot, completely Screen-Enclosed area that is dedicated to the raising of Swallowtail, Sulphur, Monarch and Gulf Fritillary butterflies.

The butterfly garden features a beautiful variety of necessary "host" plants such as; Pipevines (host for the Swallowtail), Milkweeds (host for the Monarch), Cassias (host for the Sulphur) and Purple Passionflowers (host for Zebra Longwing and Gulf Fritillary) plus several of the various colorful nectar plants that these particular butterflies feed on; Penta, Lantana, Porterweed, and more.

If You Plant It, They Will Come

View of the front of the house with Vinca and Periwinkles in bloom

Because the house has a screened area, we thought it would be an ideal place for a butterfly sanctuary

We started by planting nectar and host plants around the house

We had the Dutchman's Pipevine inside with trellises for them to climb, not realizing that the caterpillars were going to eat them all!

How We Got Started

We didn't wake up one day and say "Let's raise butterflies!"

It started with me planting flowers in the yard and noticing an occasional butterfly. My Vince has always liked butterflies, so he did some research on the internet to see how we could improve the butterfly population around our house. The more we read, the more we became intrigued with the Pipevine Swallowtail. They are called Pipevine because that is the name of the plant the butterflies use as a host (where they lay their eggs.) The plants are sometimes hard to find and not all nurseries carry them. We called several nurseries before we found Bayshore Garden Center. The owners seemed very knowledgeable about plants and butterflies, so we bought our first two Dutchman's Pipevine from them. When I asked about how the butterflies would find us, both Ken Ellam and Cinda Layton told us "If you plant it, they will come."

Since it turned out to be true, that is what I decided to name my book.

Bird of Paradise

I just love this Bird of Paradise. But, I have to admit, it was here when we bought the house, so I didn't plant it myself. I read that it does attract butterflies and since it is a bright color, I'm sure that is true. However, I don't know of any butterfly that uses it for a nectar or host plant, I just enjoy it for its beauty.

The Plants:

Plant the flowers that butterflies feed on. I read in a brochure, published by The Florida Museum of Natural History, that there are some 2800 native plants and more than 180 species of butterflies in Florida. Because of the temperature, we can pretty much enjoy butterflies all year round. There are many different nectar plants (what the butterflies eat,) so we had to pick and choose what grows best in this area. Butterflies can't regulate their body temperature very well, so if you situate your butterfly garden in a sheltered area that receives at least six hours of direct sunlight, it will give them a place to bask in the warm sunshine. The more nectar plants you have, the better your chances of having a variety of butterflies visit your garden.

You should read up on your local butterfly plants and plant the ones you think you may enjoy around your house. I always like the ones that are the easiest to take care of. Just remember, a nectar plant will usually attract bees as well, so if you have an allergic reaction to bee stings, keep them at a safe distance from the house. You may also want to plant host plants to insure new generations of butterflies. But, keep in mind, the host plant is a food source and will be eaten. Some people would rather not have the caterpillars eating all their garden plants.

I am not really a gardener, so I had a "trial and error" period before I found the plants strong enough to survive our drought conditions and thrive in sandy soil. That is why I decided to plant; Milkweed, Pentas, Lantanas, Mexican Petunias, Hibiscus, Pipevine and Porterweed. Except for the Pipevine and Milkweed, these are all nectar plants. The Milkweed serves as both a nectar and a host plant. The Pipevine is a host plant only.

As far as design, there are plenty of nurseries that will help you select plants that will thrive in your area. You may want to plant both perennial and annual plants so you have flowers all year long. Here are the things that worked for us. We planted both annuals and perennials, we varied the colors and height of the plants because butterflies are attracted to a flower's color, smell and nectar. At first, we spread our flowers out, but found butterflies were more attracted to the larger groups of flowers that were planted in the front of the house. The more flowers you have, the more likely butterflies will explore your yard.

In several of the pictures, you will see a rain barrel. This helped us tremendously. If you are feeding a lot of caterpillars, you will need a lot of plants. We have long periods where we get very little rain and you can run up quite a water bill if you don't use some sort of reservoir to supplement your watering. I'm afraid, the caterpillar's appetite became my theme throughout the book because, it seems as though, I was always scrambling to get more plants to feed them. But, since this book really isn't about gardening, that is all I am going to say along those lines. Gardening is a whole area unto itself and there are tons of books just about that one subject. I will be talking about what I had to do to keep my "food supply" going. Supporting the caterpillars is what really forced me to learn more about plants and how to keep them growing. I also had to learn a little about insects that eat our particular plants and how to enrich the soil. So, I guess you could say "raising butterflies turned me into a quasi gardener."

This is the back yard rain barrel

This is the front yard rain barrel

If You Plant It, They Will Come

A shot of the area around the house and inside the breezeway. It turned out to be the perfect place for raising butterflies!

If You Plant It, They Will Come

Flowers In Our Garden

"Flowers seem intended for the solace of ordinary humanity"

~ John Ruskin

Although the butterflies seemed to like the red Pentas, as you can see, they also enjoyed nectar from the pink Pentas too. These plants are annuals and are a Spring - Fall bloomer. They require watering two or three times a week and do attract butterflies. I keep them inside the sanctuary to feed the new butterflies until they are released, but I also have them outside for passers-by.

The Firebush is a great nectar plant and it can tolerate drought conditions. That makes it a good plant for this area. Once it has been established;it will continue to grow in full sun, partial sun and even shady areas. Since the Swallowtails seem to like this plant, I put it next to a Dutchman's Pipevine. Once the female lays her eggs on the Pipevine, she can have an afternoon snack before moving on.

The flowers in the foreground are Butterfly Weed. They look almost identical to Milkweed with the exception of the narrower leaf. They seem to be more popular at the nurseries and I frequently have to buy it for our caterpillar food source. Because of the narrower leaf, the caterpillars have to eat more of it and it doesn't last as long as the Milkweed, so it is never my first choice.

Lantanas do very well in this hot, dry area. They come in a variety of colors and serve as a nectar plant for a number of butterflies. All four types of butterflies we raise, enjoy this flower. I put them in my hanging pots and plant them both inside and outside. You need nectar plants to attract the butterflies as well as host plants for them to lay their eggs on and feed the resulting caterpillars.

The Mexican Petunia is a fast growing, flowering plant that attracts many butterflies and bees. They do particularly well in the Southwestern Florida climate where we live. They also root quickly from cuttings and are easily moved. When I read that they were a good plant for beginning gardeners, I was in. They are perennial (only have to be planted once and continue to bloom) and require little care.

The Vinca propagates very quickly and these plants do well in four to six hours of sunlight with watering two to three times a week. Although these are usually planted in the ground, I have planted some in well-drained pots inside the breezeway as well. I didn't see them listed as a butterfly plant, but several of the different species seem to like them as a nectar plant.

The Jonquil is grown from a bulb and usually flowers in the spring. It should be planted in a sunny spot with six hours of sunlight. Because it likes sandy soil, it does quite well here. The other plus is that it generally needs little water other than rainfall. If it is unusually dry, it will need water if the top two or three inches of soil is dry. This is not listed as a butterfly plant, but it does get their attention.

This Hydrangea is considered a decorative plant, but our butterflies seem to land on it a lot. It isn't one of their host or nectar plants, so I'm not sure why they are attracted to it. It is a hearty bush and beautifies the garden. It is easy to care for and only needs to be watered weekly, but during a drought, it should be watered more often. It will survive in full sun or partial shade.

Hibiscus

Almost all the butterflies like the flowers of the Hibiscus. I was told that this plant would really flourish here, but ours didn't seem to be thriving as well as I had hoped. I was expecting a hedge by now!

Dutchman's Pipevine

I had this Pipevine five months before I even knew it produced a flower. I have not had any luck with cuttings, but was able to grow some plants from seeds that were ordered on the internet.

Senna is a winter bloomer

The Senna or Cassia (some gardeners use the names interchangeable) can tolerate a host of different soil types. Because it enjoys full sun with moderate water, it does well in this area. It is also a host and nectar plant for a variety of Sulphur butterflies. I have even seen several tree versions that grow quite nicely too.

Dutchman's Pipevine Flower

The flower on the Dutchman's Pipevine is so exotic, it looks like it belongs in a rain forest. Although the Pipevine is the only plant the Swallowtail caterpillar will eat, the flower itself is not a nectar flower for the butterfly. Its only purpose seems to be to provide beauty; the caterpillars enjoy eating it. Dessert maybe?

Purple Passionflower

This beautiful Purple Passionflower is the host plant for Florida's state butterfly, the Zebra Longwing. We just planted these this year, in hopes of getting the female's attention. So far, they seem like a great plant for this area because they can tolerate full sun. However, they do require regular watering during the summer months, so the jury is still out until we see how well our new plants do this summer.

Close-up of Porterweed

Porterweed is considered a weed by some and they can certainly get out of hand because they don't require a lot of water or good soil. I found it to be very versatile and I was able to plant it inside my sanctuary in hanging pots as well out in the yard. I have seen Monarchs, Swallowtails, Sulphurs and Long-winged Skippers on this particular plant.

Close-up of Yellow and Pink Lantana

For nectar, Lantana is my plant of choice. It thrives with little moisture and in full, unyielding sun. In fact, I planted mine in an area that had been covered with rock salt to remove a stump. I was told nothing would grow there, but my Lantana is thriving with ease. It is covered with brightly colored flowers all summer and fall, and butterflies of all types are very attracted to it. They come in a multitude of colors and they are all beautiful and easy to grow.

Raising Butterflies "The Basics"

A butterfly lights beside us like a sunbeam
And for a brief moment its glory and beauty
belong to our world.
But then it flies again
And though we wish it could have stayed...
We feel lucky to have seen it.

~ Author Unknown

If You Plant It, They Will Come

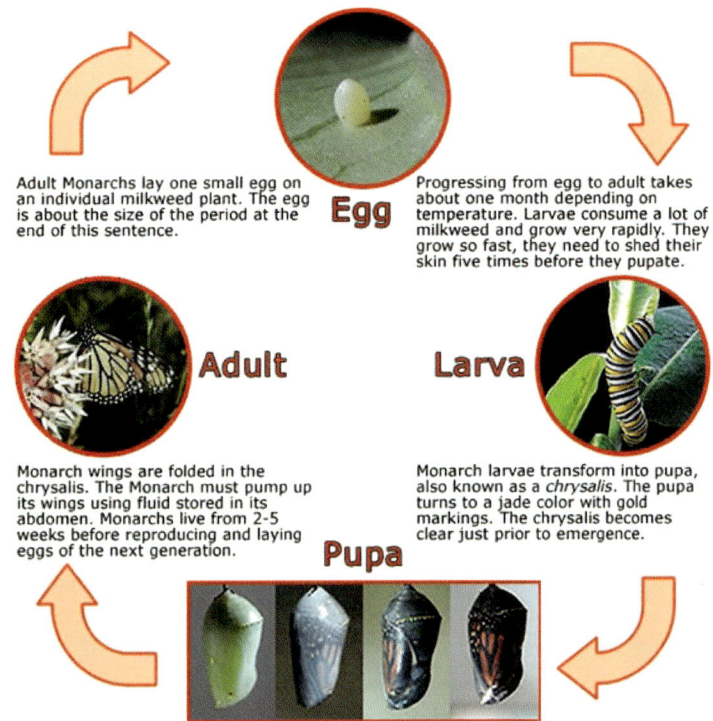

I found this life cycle on the internet at TheButterflySite.com and it takes us full circle from egg to butterfly. I use the terms caterpillar and chrysalis throughout the book instead of larva and pupa. Although many of the articles I read use Latin for the names of butterflies, flowers and plants, I prefer not to because, I'm just an ordinary person raising butterflies for the fun of it. I don't sell them, but I do sometimes delight the neighbors when I release several at a time or give tours to their grandchildren.

Graphics by http://www.TheButterflySite.com

If You Plant It, They Will Come

Our Own Life Cycle Page

These pictures were taken by Vince DeMattia. He captured the egg, caterpillar, chrysalis and the adult butterfly of the three butterfly species we raise. We added the Gulf Fritillary in 2012. I love this page because it shows how diverse the three species are, but they still live in harmony as we raise and release them.

Polydamas Swallowtail

Orange-barred Sulphur

Monarch

Raising Butterflies:

If you want to raise butterflies, find out which ones are in your area and what plant is the nectar and/or host plant for those butterflies. We found the plants the butterflies get their nectar from are not necessarily the plants they lay their eggs on; so we also had to plant "host" plants for the larva (caterpillar) to eat. I found it is best to leave the host plant in a pot because once the butterfly lays an egg, you can bring it inside until the caterpillar emerges. This will protect it from any predators. You may prefer to clip the leaves instead and put them in a container with a wet paper towel and water to keep it fresh.

Swallowtail caterpillar climbing up the door, looking for a good spot to form a chrysalis

Butterflies were popping up unexpectedly

First, I used caulking to seal all open areas around the breezeway. Because we had an enclosed area, I thought that was all I needed to do, but NO. I had no idea the caterpillars were going to start wandering around looking for a place to form their chrysalis, but that is exactly what happened. Before I knew it, I had caterpillars crawling on the screen, the table, the chairs, you name it. I actually started losing them because they were finding hiding places or other ways to get out of the breezeway. We constantly had to watch for caterpillars because they liked to hang out on the steps and risked a chance of getting stepped on. So, you either have to invest in a "Caution, Caterpillar Crossing" sign, or use that as a valid reason to purchase a cage for the caterpillars. The caterpillar containers come in all sizes, so if you just wanted to raise a few butterflies, you can get a small container and keep it in the house or on the porch.

Swallowtail chrysalises hanging on an artificial plant - my Chrysalis tree! *Monarch chrysalises around the pot - My chrysalis condos* *Caterpillar Castle with chrysalis and caterpillars*

Vince went back to the internet and found a Caterpillar Castle to purchase. Ours is a 3x4 foot net enclosure with a clear plastic "viewing" window. They come in a variety of sizes, but we have limited space. It turned out to be perfect and really did the job. To avoid stepping on the caterpillars, I put them in the Caterpillar Castle either on a small plant, or on cuttings submerged in water. I only do this when they get larger and look like they are ready to shed for the last time; this keeps them from wandering. Before I got the castle, I had a row of 5 chrysalises hanging on the lip of a pot. Fortunately, they all decided to stay in one spot and I didn't have to go searching for them.

Then I had an artificial plant that I called my Chrysalis tree. If you look closely, the brown things that look like dried leaves (or little sea horses) on the far left are Swallowtail chrysalises.

The greenish acorn-shaped ones decorated in gold are Monarchs. I had a total of 30 chrysalises when these pictures were taken.

Once the butterflies emerge, I keep them in the castle just until the wings are fully extended and dry. From there, I release them into the breezeway where I have nectar plants. They stay in the breezeway for a day or two before I let them go back to nature to start the whole process all over again.

I have tried keeping butterflies inside the breezeway, hoping they would mate and lay eggs, but ours never did. They just started getting weaker and had a hard time flying, so now, I just release them and collect the eggs from the yard. That works just fine for me and the butterflies appreciate it too.

Some caterpillars choose to form a chrysalis on their host plant, but the majority of them leave the plant searching for a nice spot to call home. I tried setting sticks in the container for them to climb on, but they really preferred an artificial plant or just attaching themselves to the ceiling of the cage. As you can tell in the picture at the bottom right, they seem to like "hanging" with their friends, much like kids of today. Even if the chrysalis is empty, a new caterpillar will still select that spot rather than contemplating another area to form its chrysalis. Maybe it takes the guess work out of it, they already know someone else thought it was a good location.

If You Plant It, They Will Come

Because the caterpillars eat so much, I couldn't afford to keep them in food if I didn't grow my own host plants. I have had the best luck with Milkweed; that is a blessing because I have so many Monarchs. My pots usually contain a stem with no leaves when the caterpillars are finished. As long as I catch them before they eat the main stem, the Milkweed will start sprouting again within a matter of days. Also, last year, I had about twenty seed pods from my older plants. That gave me quite a supply of seeds and I was able to share some of them with our Garden Club. I have planted some seeds right in the ground and others, I have placed in a soaked paper towel in a dish. Those, I kept watered every day until the seed sprouted, then I put them in the ground or in a pot. Milkweed cuttings grow roots within a few days and if you can use a cutting, you already have a head start with a new plant.

Milkweed from my own seed pods. These are ready to be separated and transferred to larger pots

These were all grown from "cuttings"

Swallowtail Butterflies

Beautiful and graceful, varied and enchanting,
small but approachable, butterflies lead you to the sunny side of life.
And everyone deserves a little sunshine.

~Jeffrey Glassberg

If You Plant It, They Will Come

Top -
Pipevine Swallowtail

Middle Right -
Zebra Swallowtail

Middle Left -
Black Swallowtail

Bottom Right - Polydamas Swallowtail

Bottom Left -
Giant Swallowtail

The Pipevine Swallowtail is almost extinct, mainly because not many people want to grow their host plant, the Dutchman's Pipevine. But, they are worth pursuing. When these beautiful Swallowtails are in the sun, the iridescent blue wings set them apart from other Swallowtails. Their wingspan is 3.25 inches. Vince took this shot while we were at The Butterfly Estates in Fort Myers, Florida.

The Black Swallowtail is really beautiful. The wingspan is also 3.25 inches and the host plant is Fennel and Dill. Until you see the underside of its wing, it looks very much like the Polydamas Swallowtail. The Black Swallowtail has two distinctive tails on the lower wings and the underside displays beautiful blue and orange dots instead of the orange and black on the Polydamas. I was able to capture this shot of the Black Swallowtail as she laid her eggs. This picture was also taken at The Butterfly Estates.

The Zebra Swallowtail is very easy to spot by the design on the wings. Their wingspan is 3.25 inches (seems to be the popular size) and their host plants are PawPaws. If you see one, it is easy to understand how it got its name. We would love to raise these, but we have no more room for host plants. This picture was taken by my Spark friend, Julie Iven.

The Giant Swallowtail is very distinctive with its 5 inch wingspan and horizontal white stripe across its back. Its host plant is citrus and although we planted a miniature citrus tree and I see a lot of these around, we have no eggs yet.

The Polydamas Swallowtail has a wingspan of 3-4 inches and flutters its wings like a hummingbird. We were lucky to get this picture right after the butterfly emerged from its chrysalis. Their host plant is the Dutchman's Pipevine and it is the only plant the caterpillar will eat. The wing color and design is beautiful.

The Eastern Tiger Swallowtail (not pictured) with a wingspan of 4-5 inches is also seen quite frequently in our neighborhood, but we don't have its host plant, the Wild Cherry, so we can only enjoy them as they fly by.

If You Plant It, They Will Come

This picture was taken at The Butterfly Estates. A low-flying Black Swallowtail and Pipevine Swallowtail, enjoying their surroundings.

Two buddies out for a road trip

As you can see, there is quite a variety of Swallowtails in Southern Florida. Oh that I could raise them all, but alas, I cannot, so I will be content with the ones we have, (unless we get lucky with the Giant Swallowtail and the Zebra Longwing.)

Both the Pipevine and the Polydamas Swallowtail use the same host plant, but the only Swallowtail species to lay eggs, so far, is the Polydamas Swallowtail. This year, we are hoping to raise two other species. Since the Zebra Longwing is the Florida state butterfly, we would especially like to be able to raise that one. We planted some Purple Passionflower, hoping to attract the Zebra Longwing and some citrus to attract the Giant Swallowtail.

Although they are all from the same family, they don't all use the same host plant. That is why you need to pick the butterflies you are trying to attract (or raise) and chose the plants you will need when planning your butterfly garden. I would need acres to plant all the host plants I would like to have.

We actually had to resort to the plants that did the best in our soil and with the weather conditions in this area. We found out in a hurry, if you can't grow the host plant, you are not going to be able to feed the caterpillars.

The Dutchman's Pipevine inside - used as our food source

When we bought these Pipevines, we were thrilled to have five Swallowtail caterpillars already on the plants. They were good sized too. However, no one told us how much they were going to eat! Within a week, we were back buying more plants. We had planted these inside the breezeway in a nice wooden planter, only to have them devoured by our hungry caterpillars. It was at this point, we decided to buy five new plants; two to put back in the planters, two to put outside and one to feed our caterpillars. The idea of putting the plants inside in the wooden planters was to use them as a food source, but only by taking clippings, letting the potted plants grow for future use. We kept the two outside plants in pots, in the event we got some eggs, we could bring the whole plant in with the eggs intact. I had never seen a Swallowtail until we put the Pipevines outside. I have no idea where it came from, but within a short time, we had a visitor. It seemed very interested in this new plant. I could see it from the window and watched it dart off several times and come back again before I realized it was a female laying eggs and maybe we should be getting some pictures. Fortunately, Vince was home and he is always willing to take pictures for me. He was able to get some good shots of what we thought was a Pipevine Swallowtail. As it turned out, this was NOT a Pipevine Swallowtail. It was a Polydamas Swallowtail. Honestly, I didn't care what it was called, it had laid eggs on our plant and we were going to be able to watch the whole life-cycle.

If you look closely at the picture on the left, you can actually see an egg starting to be placed on the plant. Unlike the Monarch, the Swallowtail will lay groups of 10 - 40 eggs on one plant. When the butterfly arches her abdomen, she is ready to lay eggs.

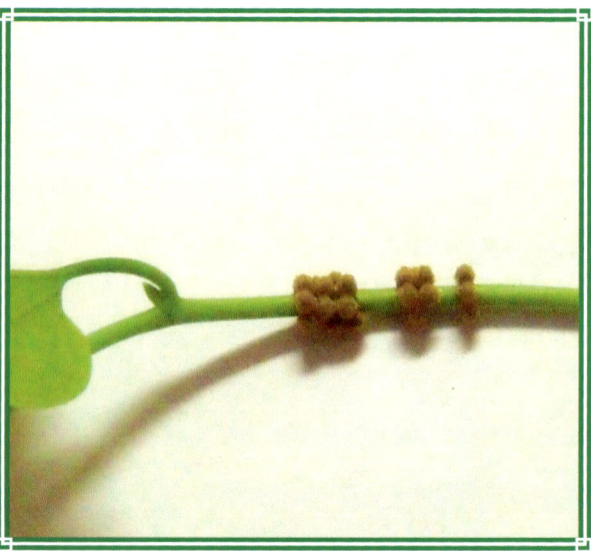

This is one of our first clumps of Polydamas Swallowtail eggs. There were twenty eggs in this first batch. Since then, I have found as many as thirty-five in one batch. So, you can see how you would use up a lot of plants to feed them. Thirty-five at one time is quite a large family to feed. Because I was rotating plants, our Pipevines were growing very nicely, but it still was always a struggle to keep up with the Swallowtail caterpillars. Growing your own food source helps tremendously.

If You Plant It, They Will Come

But wait, I'm getting ahead of myself! I didn't tell you about our original five caterpillars. Remember, we had no real idea what we were doing. We brought our two Pipevine plants home and just put them inside the breezeway. The caterpillars were already big enough to be healthy eaters and after seeing how much they ate, we were actually shocked. Those Pipevines were twenty dollars each and within four days, I saw that we were going to need more plants. That is when we came up with the idea of rotating the plants. Well, we wanted to start with Swallowtails and we were happy to get a jump start by already having caterpillars on our plants, we just weren't prepared for the immediate devastation of the entire plant. Since we didn't have a cage yet, as the caterpillars decided to leave their host plant, they were able to wander at will. Out of the five; one immediately went missing, only a few days later, I saw one covered with ants, so it died. The third one also died because it got stepped on.

Our very first Swallowtail caterpillar - "Scooter"

So, that left two. Those two did make it to the chrysalis stage and we had a chance to see what the chrysalis looked like. To me, it looked like a dried brown leaf, or kind of like a sea horse, with little ears and a nose.

A Swallowtail chrysalis

Now we had two chrysalises and no idea how long it was going to take before we actually saw a butterfly. It seemed like two or three weeks later when I walked into the breezeway and there was a butterfly on the inside of the screen. I started looking around and saw the empty chrysalis, but I had missed the whole "coming out" process. At least I had a new group of eggs to watch from the very beginning.

31

If You Plant It, They Will Come

Pipevine Swallowtail - The one we THOUGHT we had

Vince took this picture of the Pipevine Swallowtail at The Butterfly Estates. Because we had Pipvines, we fully expected to have these butterflies in our sanctuary, but it hasn't happened yet.

Polydamas Swallowtail - These are our butterflies

We have had lots of the Polydamas Swallowtail butterflies lay eggs on our Pipevines and they are beautiful. We were fortunate to catch these just after coming out of the chrysalis.

Polydamas Swallowtail fresh from the Chrysalis

Although it was our intention to attract Pipevine Swallowtails, the ones that chose to lay their eggs on our Pipevine plants are called Polydamas Swallowtails. Since I didn't know the difference, for quite a while, I was calling our butterflies Pipevine Swallowtails.

Polydamas Swallowtail ready to be released

Once I saw a picture of our black, white and orange butterfly, I made the correction. They flutter their wings like a hummingbird and are difficult to photograph in flight. I love these beautiful creatures, so I am happy with the ones we have. The caterpillars are quite cute too.

Two-days old - tiny little Swallowtail caterpillars fresh from their eggs

They seem very social and enjoy hanging out with each other

Before we got the cage

What a cutie

They spend their entire day eating as much as possible in order to grow and start their metamorphosis. Once they are ready, they start looking for a place to secure their chrysalis. Not a good idea to let them roam around the breezeway.....you never know where you will find them. This is actually our front door.

All day, every day, all these guys do is eat and eliminate waste. That was another reason we had to get the Caterpillar Castle. Ours is a 3x4 foot net cage with a plastic window in the front. I spent many hour viewing these babies through that plastic window.

If You Plant It, They Will Come

Two Monarch Chrysalises on the left and three Polydamas Swallowtail butterflies

Polydamas butterfly with empty chrysalis, beautiful wing design

New Polydamas Swallowtail with abdomen still enlarged - fluid is still pumping to the wings

One Swallowtail caterpillar and one chrysalis

If You Plant It, They Will Come

Only two days old - "Wagons Ho!"

About seven days old and still mingling

At first, we had lots of Polydamas Swallowtails, mainly because they lay their eggs in large clumps of 10-30 or more. The tiny caterpillars emerged within four or five days and I had an opportunity to observe them from the very beginning of their life. I literally spent hours watching them crawl around and eat. Of course, I had no other comparison, but these tiny little beings immediately became my favorites and still are today. What I like about them is the fact that they are so "social". From the day they come out of their eggs, they stay together in groups. If one decides to make a move, the others follow along in a "wagon train" line of caterpillars. Although they are not furry, they look like little brown bears to me. I can almost hear them saying "High-ho, high-ho, off to work we go." (I do have a vivid imagination)

The Swallowtails were affected the most by the change in the weather. When we had our first cold spell, I had twelve Swallowtail chrysalises. Normally, it only took ten to fourteen days for the butterfly to emerge, but once it got colder, the butterfly inside the chrysalis seemed to go into hibernation. It started in November and the last of those chrysalises did not produce butterflies until April of the following year. I guess that is the cycle they follow in the North and they just adopted it when the weather turned cold down here. I think Swallowtail caterpillars are the ones that created the term "social butterfly" because they really seem to enjoy hanging out together.

These caterpillars are thirteen days old and still like to stick together. They really do not mind climbing over each other and sharing their meals together.

Sharing a vine; no problem

Hard to tell where one ends and the other begins

Our Chrysalis Tree

When the weather got colder, I brought this artificial plant into the house and called it my "Chrysalis Tree", it was December and seemed very appropriate. We had a total of sixteen chrysalises on this one artificial plant. I did have one Swallowtail emerge on Christmas Eve and one on Christmas Day, but the others waited until March and April.

It is almost the end of April and I have only seen two Swallowtails so far this year. I had released two of my own earlier this month...hmmmm, coincidence? Because this has been a bad year for mosquitos, I think the Swallowtails got caught in the quest to rid our area of those pesky insects. It was just too ironic that there were no more Swallowtails laying eggs on our Dutchman's Pipevine. Although the spray is not supposed to harm butterflies, I know it does kill the caterpillars because I brought in some leaves without washing them and when I put my caterpillars on them, some did die. So, you always need to be conscious about washing plants from nurseries and washing plants that you know have been sprayed.

It is hard to believe that these beautiful butterflies came out of those shriveled brown chrysalises. These two emerged last Spring. When I no longer saw them flying around, I really missed them.

If You Plant It, They Will Come

The gold band on the head, as seen in the first picture, is what distinguishes the Polydamas Swallowtail caterpillar from the Pipevine Swallowtail caterpillar. It is also a defense mechanism that "inflates" when they are startled, staying inflated for only a few seconds. Because the caterpillars get so used to me moving them around, I don't startle them any more so it actually took several days to capture the inflated band showing in the second picture, making this picture one of our favorites.

The yellow between the horns is the gold band

It inflates to show an additional pair of horns to scare away any predators

Back in July of 2010, all we had were Swallowtails. We really were happy to start out with such a beautiful butterfly and it was amazing to be in such close proximity to them. Although they didn't land on us in the beginning, as time passed, they became more accustomed to having us around.

We had plenty of space for them to flutter about and lots of nectar plants to sustain them. These are our first butterflies. They didn't understand the concept of the screen and I felt it was torture for them to feel like they were free, but not be able to fly away. The Swallowtail caterpillars were the most social, but the Swallowtail butterflies seemed to have lost their social graces; all they really wanted was to get outside. The next generation was better adjusted to being inside.

Sulphur Butterflies

May the wings of the butterfly kiss the sun
And find your shoulder to light on,
To bring you luck, happiness and riches
Today, tomorrow and beyond.

~Irish Blessing

If You Plant It, They Will Come

The Sulphur butterfly eggs are so tiny, it is easy to miss them, unless you are a wasp. The Cassia plant is very protective of these tiny caterpillars because the leaves literally close up making a little crease for the tiny new caterpillar to nestle in and be safe at night.

A tiny Sulphur egg is on the right side of the top leaf. Our Sulphur butterflies seem to have a hard time just getting through the stages of transformation. From the minute the egg is laid, wasps are in search of them. Now, as soon as I see eggs on a plant, I bring them into the house, so I have increased the Sulphur population in this area by quite a margin.

The two tiny yellow caterpillars on the top right are three and seven days old respectively. They are yellow when they come out of the egg and really are hard to see, especially if they are right on the vein or bud of a new leaf. When they mature, like the ones above, they change in color and blend more closely with the stems and mature leaves.

Once they start growing, they really strip the leaves of the Cassia plant. These guys are only about a day away from going into the Caterpillar Castle.

I like to leave them out in the breezeway, but if they look like they are ready to leave their host plant, I will put them in the container. That way, I can keep track of them and know they are safe.

A couple of cool "cats" whiling away the afternoon

When we first started raising Sulphur butterflies, I had twelve of them in the Caterpillar Castle, all at one time. It was such a trip to watch them because my only frame of reference had been Swallowtail caterpillars and they were quite different. The Sulphur caterpillars didn't seem to really like each other and didn't travel together at all. Maybe it is because the eggs of a Sulphur are laid one at a time and the little caterpillar is on its own from the very beginning. Where the Swallowtails didn't mind sharing a leaf or branch, the Sulphur caterpillars didn't like sharing at all. They didn't seem to even be able to pass each other without striking out or "nipping" at each other before they got by. Honestly, I witnessed actual "head butting" when two caterpillars came together face-to-face. It was really hysterical and I could spend many hours just watching their antics.

Most of the caterpillars will roll in a ball when they are disturbed, but when I had to move a Sulphur from one plant to another, they would bend in half and spring open like a jack knife. The first time it happen, it startled me so much, I dropped the caterpillar. I'm a lot larger than any of their predators, so I would think that trick would scare off their enemies. It worked for me. The next time, I just let the caterpillar climb onto the new plant by itself.

If You Plant It, They Will Come

What's with all the letters? "J" for Monarchs and "U" for the Sulphur, "C" for Swallowtails

When each species of caterpillar forms its "letter" shape, It is ready to make a chrysalis

They eliminate any waste before forming the chrysalis (notice the streaks)

The Sulphur chrysalis truly blends with its surrounding, they look like green leaves

Our very first Orange-barred Sulphur butterfly

They blend with the flowers for protection

If You Plant It, They Will Come

A beautiful little lady, (I think!)

Vince captured this fantastic picture of the Orange-barred Sulphur gathering nectar from the pink Lantana. The Orange-barred Sulphur is such a delicate little butterfly. It is amazing to me that they come from such large and striking caterpillars.

I have had some very light yellow butterflies that come from the same kind of chrysalis and I think they are the Cloudless Sulphur, but to tell you the truth, I'm just guessing. I can't really tell them apart because, not all Orange-barred Sulphurs have orange on the bottom of their wings. The caterpillars are very similar too,

There are two other species of Sulphur butterflies, but only the Cloudless and the Orange-barred Sulphur use the Cassia/Senna as their host plant.

As I mentioned, our Sulphur butterflies always seem to have a hard time making it to the adult butterfly stage. First, wasps seem to love the eggs and I have to rescue as many as possible. Even inside the breezeway, they have been attacked by ants or other predators. I couldn't take the whole bush into the house, so I just cut off some of the branches with eggs and brought them in. I put them in a container with fresh water and watched them every day. When the caterpillars arrived, I waited for several days for them to get big enough to put on fresh branches. I continued doing this for about two weeks. I started with eight caterpillars and one day I noticed there were only five. I looked closely and to my horror, there were three dead caterpillars at the bottom of the jar. I was mortified. I had tried so hard to keep them alive only to have them drown themselves in a jar of water. Next, I put the branches in a bottle with a small opening and taped the top closed so they couldn't get in the water. Wouldn't you know it, one morning one caterpillar was dead, having gotten stuck to the tape. Now I was down to four and I wasn't taking any chances. I put a whole bush inside the breezeway with my four remaining caterpillars. That did the trick. They finally got large enough to put inside the Caterpillar Castle on an artificial plant. They successfully formed chrysalises and turned into four beautiful Orange-barred Sulphur butterflies. My goodness, what a journey! But, I still had a fifty percent survival rate and that is a heck of a lot better than the two percent rate I read about.

If You Plant It, They Will Come

After their difficult struggle to get to the adult butterfly stage, I didn't want to let these little beauties go. I actually kept them for a few days, but because their life span is so short, I felt they needed their freedom more than I needed to keep them in captivity.

Monarch Butterflies

I've watched you now a full half-hour
Self-poised upon that yellow flower
And, little Butterfly! Indeed
I know not if you sleep or feed.
How motionless! - not frozen seas
More motionless! and then
What joy awaits you, when the breeze
Hath found you out among the trees, And calls you forth again!

~William Wordsworth, "To a Butterfly"

If You Plant It, They Will Come

I love how the light reflects through the wings of these beautiful Monarchs. These pictures were taken when my friend, Jennifer Knoll, came to visit. She is like this wonderful butterfly. She flies in from time to time to pay a visit and I cherish every moment of her stay.

If You Plant It, They Will Come

I grew up in the country. Living in Idaho, I learned to appreciate nature and I even remember finding caterpillars and chrysalises that turned into butterflies. But, it wasn't until moving to our home in Florida that I ever thought about raising butterflies myself.

Maybe it had something to do with retiring and having more time to pursue other things. I am just so happy to have had this experience. I really don't know which I enjoy more, the butterflies or the caterpillars because they are all quite unique.

Before we bought the Caterpillar Castles, it really was a lot more work because I was always cleaning up after the caterpillars. I still have a lot to do, but the space is more confined and it is a lot faster and easier to clean the containers than it is to clean the whole breezeway.

Now, the gardening is the most time-consuming aspect because we go through drought conditions that require a lot of extra watering time. I need to keep the plants in good health because, between Monarch, Swallowtail and Sulphur butterflies, I have had as many as forty-three chrysalises all at one time. You can imagine how many plants the caterpillars ate before forming all those chrysalises. I am constantly working in the garden; weeding, planting, ridding plants of; aphids, ants, milkweed bugs and spiders. As I mentioned, I keep a lot of the host plants in pots so I can move them inside the breezeway and Caterpillar Castle. Therefore, I like to root plants and start new pots to keep the inventory going.

It isn't necessary to put the caterpillars inside the Caterpillar Castle until they get a little larger. When they are small, they don't eat as much and they stay right on their host plant. As they grow, they start storing up for their metamorphosis and they go through plants quite quickly. It is during this time that they eliminate a lot of waste and I need to clean the cage at least once a day.

If You Plant It, They Will Come

A handful of beautiful butterflies

Crushed in a wanting grasp

A handful fluttering in the air

Free to show their beauty and grace

Which is more beautiful?

Grasping to hold?...or to behold?"

~Andrew Hawkes

Just so you know how inexperienced we were when we started raising butterflies; I thought these were eggs. I was so excited because I thought I had hit the jackpot, but when they started moving, something just didn't seem right. So, we took a picture and e-mailed it to our local nursery. They laughingly told us these were aphids, not eggs. Not only was I embarrassed, I also realized that we had an infestation problem. I literally went around and wiped off each plant by hand because I didn't want to spray anything that might harm the butterflies or caterpillars. I had heard a flower expert talk about using liquid Dawn or Dove in a spray bottle to rid your plants of aphids. I sprayed each plant and then watered them really well to get the soap off. That seemed to temporarily take care of the problem. The second year, I had nothing like what you see in the picture. But, in year three, they came back with a vengeance. We read an article about ladybugs and have decided to use them to help with the aphids. That is nature's way of getting rid of the pests. Besides, who doesn't like ladybugs? They will arrive soon and we will see how that works.

If You Plant It, They Will Come

Monarch Egg

This is what a real Monarch egg looks like. The female lays her eggs one at a time, usually on the underside of a Milkweed leaf. It only takes about four days for the caterpillar to emerge. The egg will turn black, showing the caterpillar head just before it breaks through the shell.

See the tiny caterpillar on the center leaf

These guys are tiny! When they come out of the egg, they immediately start eating; first their egg, then the leaf they are on. This is my incubator for the eggs. Any container will do. A damp paper towel keeps the leaves fresh. Place the leaves inside with the egg side up.

Look closely, they are really tiny

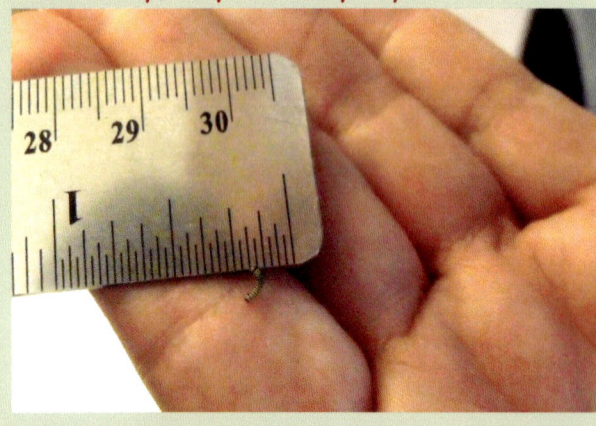

I check my plants each day and my eyes have become accustomed at spotting these tiny babies. I have host plants in pots as well as in the garden. I remove the caterpillars from the garden by hand to put them on one of the potted plants, or I clip the leaf with the egg and put it in my incubator. That way, I can keep them inside the screened area.

Lots of hungry caterpillars

This also prevents them from eating all my outside plants. I need those to attract and feed the Monarch butterflies. You can see from this picture, the caterpillars grow quite quickly and eat continuously. That is their only purpose, eat, grow and turn into a butterfly. So, growing your own plants becomes a necessity.

52

If You Plant It, They Will Come

From new egg to tiny caterpillar

    We were lucky enough to catch an egg within days of being laid. When the Monarch first deposits her egg on the leaf, it is nice and white, like any other egg, as seen in the first photo. In the second and third photos, you can clearly see a black spot on the top of the egg. That is the head of the tiny caterpillar.

    In the fourth picture, you have to squint a little, but you can actually see the outline of a tiny caterpillar down the right side of the egg. Within four days, the tiny, tiny caterpillar on the vertical leaf in picture number five emerged. It had already eaten its egg when this picture was taken.

    The fifth and sixth pictures also show a comparison between a day old caterpillar and one that is four days old. They are still growing pretty slowly at this stage, but at the end of the next week, they get bigger by the day.

    The little incubators I made and started using, really gave Vince an opportunity to capture pictures of the eggs and tiny babies right from the beginning.

If You Plant It, They Will Come

Looking at these pictures will give you an idea about how much these little guys eat. If you let them, they will kill the plant, so the idea is to let them eat all the leaves, then move them to another plant before they eat the whole stem. They grow so quickly they need to shed their skin four or five times before starting to form the chrysalis. I have read different numbers, but the formation of the chrysalis is usually the fourth or fifth shedding of the skin. I remember seeing skins on the ground or on leaves and thinking my caterpillars had died - Always the worrier!

Here, I am actually gathering the caterpillars from the plant they have devoured and physically moving them to a new plant.

The last picture tells me this caterpillar is starting to look for a place to form its chrysalis. I will be moving it into the Caterpillar Castle today.

Several formed chrysalises and three caterpillars in the "J" position

When several of them are eating, I can actually hear them munching.

The caterpillar's only function is to eat and morph into a butterfly

These future Monarch butterflies are safe and snug inside their castle and will remain there until the butterfly emerges from the chrysalis. They really switch into high gear and eat non-stop when they are getting ready to start their transformation. A good indication that they are ready to leave the host plant is when the leaves are gone or you see them circling the edge of the pot. But, this could also mean that they are still hungry and looking for more food.

If they really are just hungry, when I change plants, the caterpillars roaming around the container will return to the plant and start eating again. So, they must know they are not quite ready yet. I try to keep enough plants so they can eat as much as they want, because the more they eat, the bigger the chrysalis, resulting in a bigger butterfly. But, when I have twenty caterpillars at a time, they can go through as many as thirteen plants before they feel ready to form a chrysalis.

Thank heavens Milkweed grows quickly. A few times, I have literally had no more plants to transfer them to and made a mad dash to the nursery, only to find they just had a few "scraggly" plants to choose from. Now, I grow my own Milkweed and have a good food supply. Because the caterpillars eat so much, I couldn't afford to keep them in food if I didn't. I have had the best luck with Milkweed and that is a blessing because I have hundreds of Monarchs.

If You Plant It, They Will Come

More pictures of how big the caterpillars get and how much they eat. Nothing tiny about any of these caterpillars!

There is nothing left of that plant on the lower left and not much on the right-hand plant either. I actually caught these just in time because they were well on their way to eating the vein of the leaf and then the stem. That would have killed the plant.

Photos by Jennifer Knoll

If You Plant It, They Will Come

No phone booth required

Just like Superman! This caterpillar changed its clothes right before our eyes - No phone booth required. If you didn't know the caterpillar sheds its skin, you too might mistake it for a dead caterpillar.

This is inside the Caterpillar castle

When the caterpillar finds the perfect spot, it attaches itself with silk and hangs in this very distinctive "J" position. They hang as if in a trance for a full day. Maybe this is a test to see if they like the spot.

Getting ready

When the chrysalis starts to form, it works its way over the whole body; creating a beautiful green and gold covering. (shown in the center of the picture)

The caterpillar "face mask"

On some of the chrysalises, I saw a black wad of something at the very top, after the chrysalis was formed. This is actually the caterpillar's skin as it was pushed to the top. It drops off all in one piece and is called a face mask. Some elementary school kids were collecting and mounting them for a school project....I'm just sayin'

57

The Making Of A Chrysalis

The caterpillar does all the work but the butterfly gets all the publicity.

~Attributed to George Carlin

If You Plant It, They Will Come

Scouting for a good location

Maybe it is because I have been in real estate, but I learned that location is everything when you are buying or selling a house. Apparently caterpillars feel the same way because, when they are getting ready to build a chrysalis, they wander around scouting for the perfect spot. They will check out a site where another caterpillar has decided to form a chrysalis and many times, build right next door.

This is the place!

In trying to get a few shots of a chrysalis being formed, I had to watch the caterpillars for a few days in a row. I thought they were very much like people, even gathering to discuss a particular location and its merits. The "point man" for the group arrived first. When the other caterpillars arrived, it really looked like they were having a conference about the location. There was already one chrysalis in place and they would crawl over to it, look around and crawl away. The next time I checked on them, all three had gathered with their heads together and it looked like they were coming to a decision. I guess they liked the location because overnight, one had already formed a chrysalis and the other three caterpillars were in the "J" position.

Within seconds, the caterpillar was disappearing

I thought I had plenty of time because they usually hold that position for almost a day before anything happens, but I didn't know when they started. I was in and out taking care of the plants; when I looked closer, I saw a green "hat" already forming on the head of one of them.

If You Plant It, They Will Come

Old skin is moving to the top

Dropping the face mask

The chrysalis starts to swing

Because we had been waiting for this, Vince already had his camera ready when I called and sure enough, within minutes, the green area started creeping up the body of the caterpillar.

If I had to compare this with something; it looked like a woman trying to squeeze into a tight pair of panty hose. It wiggled and moved like it was struggling to pull the garment up. Instead of being long and skinny, the body started getting fatter and shorter. The chrysalis continues to move up over the body and the skin is actually being shed. You can still see the antenna as they are being pushed up to the top of the chrysalis.

The dark bunch at the top of this chrysalis is actually the remains of the last shedding. It falls off all in one piece and is called the face mask. (shown on an earlier page)

As it became more compact, the bottom of the chrysalis became smooth, but the top still had ripples in it.

When I looked closely, I could still see the stripes of the caterpillar in the top half of the chrysalis. I could tell this process was really a lot of work for the caterpillar because, it didn't just wiggle, it gyrated almost creating a centrifugal force to urge the covering up and over its body.

If You Plant It, They Will Come

Gyrating the chrysalis

One finished, one ready to go

The Location was unanimous, all 5 decided to build here

At one point it started to look like a large Lima bean and it shook so violently, the top of the cage moved. It changed right before my eyes and still shook, but with lapses of rest in between wiggles.

At this stage, you can still see the outline of the caterpillar's body, but it is already starting to change. This is when the true transformation starts to take place. The caterpillar kind of melts down to form an embryo-type fluid that is the beginning of the butterfly.

From start to finish, it took fifty-two minutes. When it was completely formed, it hung perfectly still. The end result was a beautiful acorn-shape with a smooth green finish. In the bottom picture, the chrysalis right in the center is the newest and not quite completely formed. The sage-colored chrysalis is the oldest and the bright green ones are still recent enough not to have changed color.

There is a very distinctive gold ring near the top and a few gold specs at the bottom of the chrysalis. If these gold adornments have any meaning, I don't know them, but it makes for a beautifully decorated shell to house a future butterfly.

Mother Nature really does know how to accessorize!

Emerging Monarch Butterfly

"If nothing in the world ever changed,
There wouldn't be butterflies."

~ Author Unknown

Emerging Monarch

We were so grateful this week because there was only one chrysalis in the castle, so it was easy to keep track of the progress. When the chrysalis becomes translucent, you can see the wings of the Monarch outlined against the sides and within twenty-four hours, it starts to break open. We caught this Monarch just as it broke through the bottom of its chrysalis. As it emerged, I thought it looked like an umbrella that is about to unfold. At first, the wings are all crumbled and it looks like the butterfly is not going to be able get them free, but once its head and front legs are out, it starts pulling the wings through. You can clearly see the large abdomen in the fourth and fifth pictures. It is filled with the fluid it takes to straighten the wings. The butterfly was turning in a circle as the fluid released and the wings slowly started to expand. They slough off any excess fluid after the wings are completely expanded.

If You Plant It, They Will Come

Extending wings to completion

As the abdomen got smaller, the wings extended. It took about forty-five minutes for the full inflation of the wings and about two hours of hanging and resting for the wings to dry and the butterfly to gain its strength. The butterfly started flexing its wings to catch some sun and that is when I took him from the castle and put him on a nectar plant in the breezeway. Caution, there is a fluid that is left behind and it must be sweet because the ants will swarm to it. They come out of nowhere so, the containers always need to be thoroughly cleaned after a release. The last picture was taken outside where the butterfly was free to start a new life.

How thrilling to have caught the very beginning of the butterfly emerging and see the whole process. It was awesome!

If You Plant It, They Will Come

This picture clearly shows the large abdomen and the liquid left in the chrysalis and on the butterfly. The liquid looks green in the picture, so I don't know if it changes color; it is a pinkish color when it hits the floor of the container. It also shows that the long flexible nose, or proboscis, is separated when the butterfly first emerges. By the time the butterfly is completely formed, the proboscis will grow together making a straw-like tool used for sucking nectar out of plants. It is designed to be able to reach deep inside the plant to search for nectar. A butterfly doesn't actually chew, it just drinks its dinner.

Hmmm, I think I have known some butterflies in my lifetime!

When we started our little sanctuary, we had visions of sitting in the breezeway, having our morning coffee with butterflies flying all around us. Well, that just didn't happen. When I first take the butterflies out of the Caterpillar Castle, I put them on a nectar plant. They will remain there and eat until they get a little stronger, but instead of flying around the breezeway, they go directly to the screen and stay there.

I was trying to figure out why our butterflies were not interested in the nectar plants we had inside the sanctuary. We even took the time to visit The Butterfly Estates in Fort Myers to see if we could learn anything new. It was after this trip that Vince installed rods for me to hang the potted plants high enough for the butterflies to see while on the screen. This helped somewhat, but unless I placed them on the plants, they didn't seem too interested.

I read somewhere that people successfully raised pairs of butterflies that mated while in captivity. So, we actually tried an experiment to see if we could get them to mate in captivity ourselves. But, that just never happened for us. We put ten butterflies inside the Caterpillar Castle with live nectar plants. There were both male and female butterflies in the cage, but they ignored each other and they wouldn't eat, so we let them out after two days. It looked like they were getting weaker and I couldn't stand to keep them contained any longer. I haven't given up though. I want to try it again with only one pair in my bigger castle and see if that makes a difference. We saw butterflies laying eggs at The Butterfly Estates, so we know that they will mate in captivity. At least I can still collect eggs from my outside plants, so it won't be a total loss if we can't get them to mate.

If You Plant It, They Will Come

To be honest with you, the only butterflies I can clearly identify between male and female are the Monarchs. The male has very distinctive black dots on the inner vein of the lower wing. They really can't be seen very clearly until the male spreads his wings like in this picture, then they become very easy to spot. It's hard to tell here, but the male is usually a little larger than the female.

Male Monarch

The female is usually, but not always, a little smaller and has no spots. If you look at her wings, the veins are a little thicker, but there are no identifying spots on the lower wing. With our last group of Monarch butterflies, the females seemed to have more brown in their pigmentation, making them a little darker than the golden-colored males.

Female Monarch

If You Plant It, They Will Come

In this picture, there are beautiful blooming plants all around, but the Swallowtails are ignoring them. We were told that butterflies are attracted to the light and that is why they go immediately to the screen. We really didn't want to darken the breezeway by installing shades or dark plastic, so we work with it the way it is. I did find, if I placed them on the nectar plants several times, they eventually started eating on their own. We still prefer to release them after a day or two. The only reason we would keep them longer than that is if the weather is bad or they have some kind of problem that prevents them from flying. When that happens, those become our household pets.

Some Butterfly Stories

Once I read a story about a butterfly in the subway, and today, I saw one. It got on at 42nd, and off at 59th, where, I assume it was going to Bloomingdales to buy a hat that will turn out to be a mistake - as almost all hats are.

~ from the film "You've Got Mail"*

* Our favorite movie

You may find this hard to believe, but it is a true story. On Friday the 13th, of this year, thirteen of our Monarchs all came out of their chrysalis within hours of each other. Here is how the story unfolded:

I have only had one or two Monarchs emerge from their chrysalis over the last two weeks, but today, I had 13 new butterflies!!! Can you believe it? I was talking to my friend, Carolyn, showing her the ten butterflies that had appeared throughout the morning and I said, it looks like two more are going to come out before the day is over. We were sitting in the breezeway talking when number 11, then number 12 decided to pay us a visit. That is the largest number I have ever had all at one time. I was really thrilled.

We watched for a while and then got back to talking. Within a few minutes, number thirteen came out of its chrysalis. I was telling her that I was happy to see that all the butterflies seemed healthy because, once in a while, they can't hang on until their wings are dry and they fall. I think I put a jinx on poor number thirteen because, I had just finished telling her that and when I looked back, the butterfly was on the floor. I rushed over, picked it up right away and put it on a plant. I was too late. I watched it for the rest of the day and the wings did not unfold. They had been damaged when it hit the floor. It must have had internal injuries too because unlucky number thirteen passed on before the sun had set. I was a little sad, but that may have been nature's way of weeding out the weaker ones. I have a dozen beautiful, strong Monarchs left and I am really excited about that. I have both male and female, so I know we are going to be starting a whole new generation. Life goes on! When we have a larger number of butterflies to release, we invite some of the neighbors over to watch the show. It really is a thing of beauty to see so many butterflies taking off all at one time. I guess that is why the latest craze is to release butterflies at weddings instead of throwing rice, like they did in my day.

A butterfly in the hand is worth ...

When our butterflies emerge from their chrysalis, we leave them in the Caterpillar Castle until their wings are completely dry. When they start fluttering around a little, we release them into the breezeway where the nectar plants are hanging in pots and blooming in planters. Because they have such a short life span, we like to release them the next morning, when the sun is warm and bright. A few days ago, Vince was helping me release the Monarchs and a strange thing happened. He will usually just hold his hand out and the butterfly will fly off, but this particular one didn't want to go. It just basked in the sun right on Vince's hand. Finally, it took off, but instead of flying away, it just circled and came right back to him. It landed on his chest and wouldn't leave. We both started laughing because it was like the butterfly was saying "Please, Dad, don't make me go." We decided to take it back inside and wait until the next day to release it. The second day, it had no problem bidding us farewell.

A butterfly in the hand is worth ...

We released this little beauty in honor of our friend and neighbor, Ray Quinton, to escort his spirit to the great beyond

Butterfly Release - Papago Tribe

If anyone desires a wish to come true they must first capture a butterfly and whisper that wish to it. Since a butterfly can make no sound, the butterfly can not reveal the wish to anyone but the Great Spirit who hears and sees all. In gratitude for giving the beautiful butterfly its freedom, the Great Spirit always grants the wish. So, according to legend, by making a wish and giving the butterfly its freedom, the wish will be taken to the heavens and be granted.

I think it is because of this saying that we are seeing more weddings and funerals that are doing butterfly releases after the ceremony. I have even released my own butterflies in honor of a departed friend or neighbor.

Sometimes You Need A Butterfly Sitter:

Who would have ever thought butterflies might need a sitter? I certainly never did, until I had to go out of town for a few days. I had more than a dozen caterpillars on a live plant in the Caterpillar Castle and at least that many chrysalises. At the rate the caterpillars were eating, there was not enough room to add an additional plant, so someone had to keep an eye on them and replace the plant after it had been eaten down so far it would have been killed. Also, when a butterfly emerges, I like to let it out into the breezeway when the wings have dried. That is where the nectar plants are located and it gives them more room to fly. Normally, we release them back into nature on the first or second day.

This ensures that they have time to find a mate and lay eggs. I'm still trying, but I have yet to get a pair to mate in captivity, so I like to release them as soon as I see they are strong and able to fly.

So, as any good parent would do, I got a butterfly sitter. We have some good friends, Carolyn and Eric Soderberg, that offered to come over and watch the butterflies. Carolyn used to raise Monarchs up in Michigan, so I knew she was a well qualified butterfly sitter. Because of them, I could leave home without any worry. They came to the house and checked on the caterpillars and chrysalises while we were away and fortunately, the "children" behaved. We have a little table and chairs, with lots of pretty flowers, so the breezeway is a nice place for people as well as butterflies. I am thankful that they were able to sit in the breezeway and enjoy themselves a little while they checked on our "kids".

So, if you are looking for a different kind of job, you might want to try butterfly sitting. It may not pay well, but it can be a lot of fun.

Not all butterflies come out of the chrysalis perfectly formed. If they are unable to fly for some reason, we keep them inside the butterfly sanctuary and let them live out their lives in luxury. I have been asked if we name all the butterflies and the answer is, No! We only name a few of them. Because we have raised so many, we only give them names if we are going to keep them as pets in the sanctuary. Case in point are Bentley and Ilene; he was born with a very bent wing that could not be straightened. She was born with a misshapen leg that caused her to lean to one side (hence, their names.) I had to assume that they were not in pain because they were normal in every other way. However, since neither could fly very well, they became my "kids"

Bently is on the left. He and Ilene are busy sucking up dinner with their proboscis. It functions like a straw and they can happily drink their dinner.

If You Plant It, They Will Come

and I took care of them inside. Both were good eaters and that is very encouraging because they will probably live to their butterfly maturity, 2 to 6 weeks is average. They are a pair, so they could surprise me and mate. That would be awesome. Both seemed to recognize me and eat right on my hand. The picture below shows my kids at dinnertime. Yes, I probably am a little crazy when it comes to my kids, but I wouldn't change a thing. I read somewhere that butterflies like honeydew melon and watermelon.

A closer look at Bentley drinking his watermelon

It turned out to be their favorite treat. I even squeezed the juice over plants as well as fixed them a dinner plate.

Since these two couldn't fly yet, I served them dinner in the breezeway.

They both eventually got strong enough and adapted to their short-comings. After about a week, we were able to release them and they flew off into the wild blue yonder. What a nice reward for me! I'm sure they will miss the room service when they are out there on their own, but now they can mate and perhaps I will see Ilene again, someday, laying eggs in the garden.

Meet Ilene, having dinner in tonight.

This was one of my worst repair jobs because I used a piece of band-aid and it was too heavy. I also had inadvertently taped the two wing portions together. When I saw that he was really having trouble flying, I decided to give it a second try. I had to put him back inside a cold glass, in order to sedate him enough to remove the band-aid. This time, I used some light tape and that did the trick. I thought I had traumatized him too much by going through the process twice, but I'm happy to tell you, he was fine. As soon as I put him out in the sun, he was able to fly with ease. One thing about doing a repair job; you can recognize your own butterflies. I actually saw this one come back to the yard several times. I'll bet he was looking for a mate. When I see a butterfly flying up to the screen and peering in, I get the feeling it is one that we have raised and released. This year, we had more and more of them flying right into the breezeway, while we were working. That used to be rare. So, I think we have had new generations of our butterflies flying around the neighborhood and coming back to where they know the food is plentiful. I also think they feel safe enough to fly right in when the doors are open. Now, that's a treasure!

If You Plant It, They Will Come

Sometimes They Need Help......

As in the case of "Maverick" and "Goose"* pictured here. One of Maverick's wings is only partially formed, so it is difficult for her to fly. As several days passed, she got stronger and did manage to fly enough to get around a good deal more... going from nectar plant to nectar plant. Maverick is a good eater, which made her stronger. (We had already named her Maverick before we realized she was a female, but we liked the name and decided to keep it.)

As for the one we called Goose, his wings formed but would not fold upward. So, he could not fly at all, but was otherwise healthy and did not seem to be in pain. Because they couldn't fly anywhere, we kept them in the house and they stayed right on the bouquet of flowers on Vince's desk. They were company for each other and didn't seem to mind being indoors at all.

*Their names were taken from one of my favorite movies "Top Gun" Maverick was the pilot and Goose was his RIO.

Who Was The Smarter One?

I put Goose on the flowers, but... he could not balance himself long enough to eat... and would fall onto the table upside-down. When I put my finger over him, he would climb up and I held him while he ate. It wasn't long before I noticed that, if he was hungry, when I came into view, he kicked himself off the flowers onto the table and would lay there until I came and got him. He got used to me picking him up so he could eat. Isn't it amazing, how he had me trained so well? These two really were my buddies and liked to hang out with me when I worked. I read that they actually can recognize you as someone that has cared for them and it seemed to be true, because they had no fear of either Vince or me and became household pets for the rest of their days.

Goose hitching a ride

Me in my gardening outfit, hanging out with Maverick

If You Plant It, They Will Come

Butterfly Love

Because we have a lot of nectar plants in the yard, butterflies frequently visit our garden. One day, I noticed what I guessed was a male Monarch, hovering on the other side of the screen, almost nose-to-nose with our female Monarch inside the screen. She didn't seem too excited, but I decided to release her anyway. Sure enough, when she flew into the air, he immediately started to chase her. Females are ready to mate upon emerging from the chrysalis, so she didn't have to look far for a mate. It must have been those wonderful pheromone that got her attention. That is how the female butterflies find the males. I've read different information about whether the male, female or both release the pheromone. However it goes, they find each other. Once released, I have seen them mate on the ground, in the trees and yes, even in mid-air. How's that for acrobatics?!

Our new little female Monarch, still inside

It was love at first sight, or should I say, sniff?

If You Plant It, They Will Come

The flowers were in bloom, the sun was shining, the sky was blue and there was love all around us!

Photos by Jennifer Knoll

My Butterfly Friends

I saw a butterfly up in the air
It originated from, I know not where
It circled, circled, all around
Then lightly landed on the ground
It climbed a plant with it's little legs
And after, eating, left some eggs
We took those eggs and watched them grow
From caterpillar to chrysalis, we loved them so
A thing of beauty for all to see
When butterflies emerged, we set them free
Far and wide they may roam
But, when they're here, they have a home
The door is open and I can see,
They clearly do remember me!

~ Cynthia Harrington ~

These two actually lived their lives inside the house

Ready to leave home

Our very first Polydamas Swallowtail

Was She Comming Home?

 I want to tell you a little story and you will realize what inspired me to write about my "*Butterfly Friends*".

I had an unusual thing happen while I was cleaning the breezeway. I had the door propped open and had seen a Monarch flying around the house. I didn't give it much thought because they are around the house all the time. I had just started weeding and watering my plants inside when this beautiful Monarch, to my utter amazement, flew right in the door, just like she lived there.
She went right up to a Milkweed plant and landed. As she flitted around checking out the plants, I closed the door. I wasn't worried about keeping her inside because we have a lot of nectar plants and she seemed very calm and right at home. She spent the rest of the day going from plant-to-plant depositing eggs. When I saw her eating, I was sure it was alright to keep her over night. The next morning, she was on the screen and seemed ready to go, so I released her and she flew away. As soon as she left, I checked my plants and found eleven eggs. I just know that she was one of our earlier releases and had come back home to lay some eggs of her own. I can't tell you, what a wonderful feeling I had that day.

Just call me "Grandma"

Came back home for a visit

She left a little present

Ready to go on her way again

If You Plant It, They Will Come

Just Too Cold To Fly

When we first started raising butterflies, I had no idea that they were cold blooded and could not fly if their body temperature was below 80-86 degrees. I had already released dozens of butterflies when I ran into that situation. This little guy looked perfectly healthy, but he could not fly. Actually, he didn't even try. He just walked around the breezeway seemingly content. He didn't even mind me picking him up, so I was kind of happy he couldn't fly. Since Swallowtails flap their wings like a hummingbird, it is unusual to get them to stay still for any long period of time. When you live in Florida, you don't expect it to ever get cold, but it did. When the temperature dropped into the low sixties, this little guy felt the change and could not fly. Of course, as soon as it got warm, the next day, we were able to release him and he flew away with only a tip of his hat and a wave Good-bye.

Just needed to take a break

She Thought I Looked Familiar

This was very strange! I was doing my warm-up walk before I started running. I was about a block from home when this Monarch butterfly circled me as I walked. She was flying very slowly, so I stopped to look at her. Sure enough, she circled me one more time and then landed on my chest. She looked pretty tired and battered, so I decided to forgo my run for a moment and take her home.

I think she may have been at the end of her life because she seemed grateful to be placed on a nectar plant inside the breezeway. I left her there all afternoon. The next morning, she looked a little stronger so I put her on a Milkweed outside in the garden. She laid one egg and flew away. I was amazed; I really do think that was the last egg of her life and she flew into the great beyond. I was pleased that she allowed me to bring her home and especially that she graced me with her final egg. Her memory will live on because the egg produced a caterpillar that became a strong male Monarch. He was released to start a family of his own and maybe we will be fortunate enough to see some of his offspring as well.

If You Plant It, They Will Come

She Was Hanging Around For A While!

Sometimes, they just don't want to leave, as in the case of this little lady. I took her outside three different times and she just would not fly away. I certainly don't force them. If they are not ready, I bring them back into the breezeway and try again later. This one seemed perfectly content to hang out on the Lantana and Penta nectar plants inside the breezeway. The next day, I was cleaning things up and I had the door open all morning. Although she could have flown out, she didn't. I was beginning to think something was wrong with her. I guess she caught my vibes because she took that moment to dart out the door and fly away.

86

If You Plant It, They Will Come

The top picture is the caterpillar of the Gulf Fritillary butterfly. On close examination, this one has a head that looks much like an ant. Its skin looks almost wet and the spines are black and bristly. Since I found the eggs at the very end of a Passionflower tendril, I wasn't surprised to learn that these caterpillars are rather aloof.

Next is the caterpillar of the Sulphur butterfly. Perhaps because these guys seem to have the toughest time surviving, they are kind of the bullies of the bunch. Their head is much more rounded and they do use it to butt other caterpillars.

The Swallowtail caterpillar looks a little intimidating with its horns and spikes, but it really is one of the most "easy going" of the group. The caterpillars emerge from a cluster of eggs and travel with that same group until they become larger "teenagers".

Lastly is the Monarch caterpillar. I probably have spent the most time with them. Although the Monarch eggs are laid separately, the caterpillars seem to crave companionship and although they don't travel in groups, they enjoy the company of others.

If You Plant It, They Will Come

OK, Get in line, time for lunch. Hey, you guys in the back, shape up!

It was too cold, so this little lady is just out for a stroll. There will be no flying today.

Sugar-water added to plants makes a special treat

She Wanted To Stay Where It Was Warm

My butterflies are feeling this little cold spell and I don't have many chrysalises left. One Monarch was in the breezeway looking like she was just freezing. I brought her in and set her on a plant inside the house. She wasn't eating, so I put some sugar-water in the microwave. I also added a spot of red food coloring just for fun and to get her attention. That makes a nice substance that I could dab on the leaves of my plant to make her want to eat. I'll tell you, she started eating like she had been in hibernation! Anyway, she is so comfortable now, I may have to adopt her.

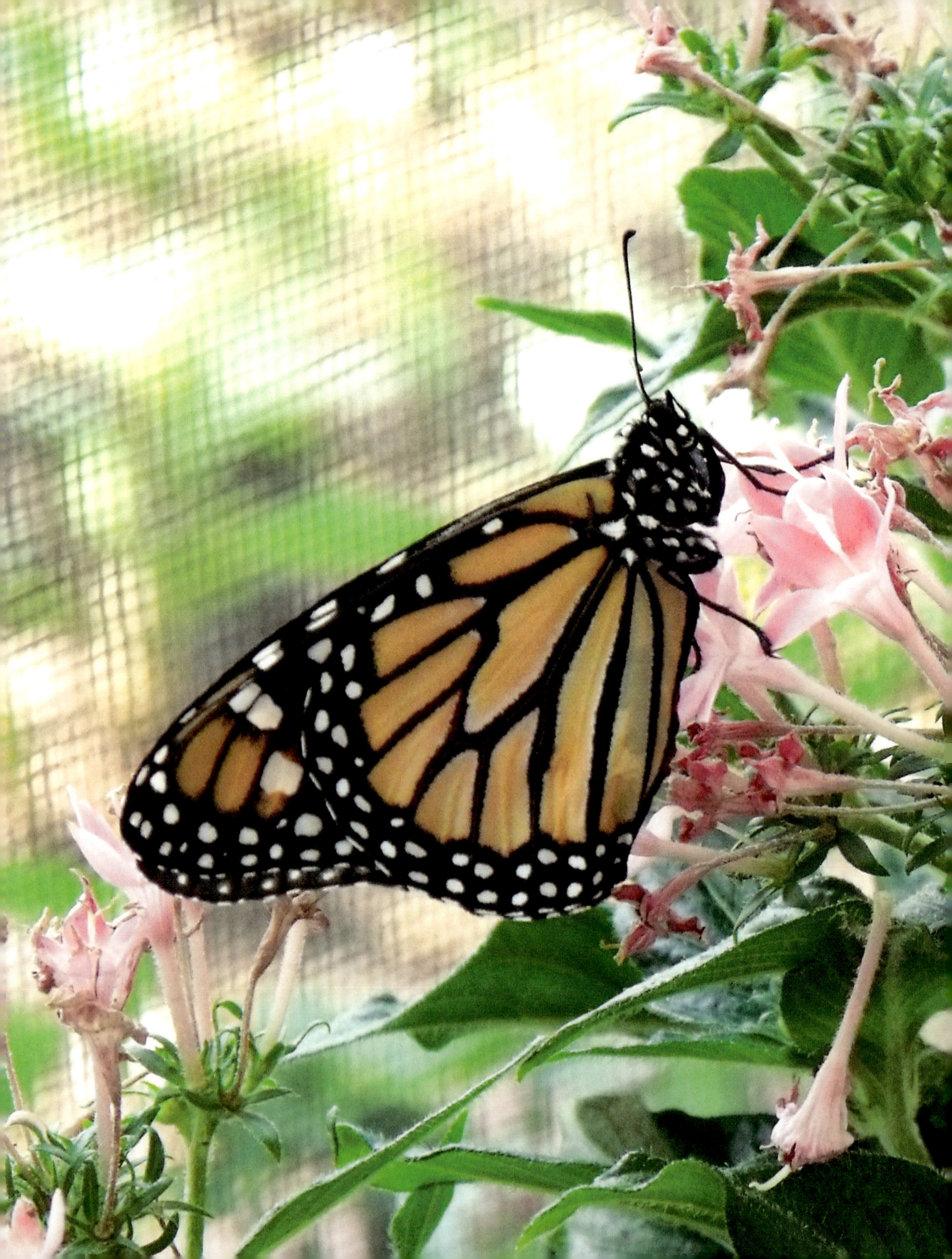

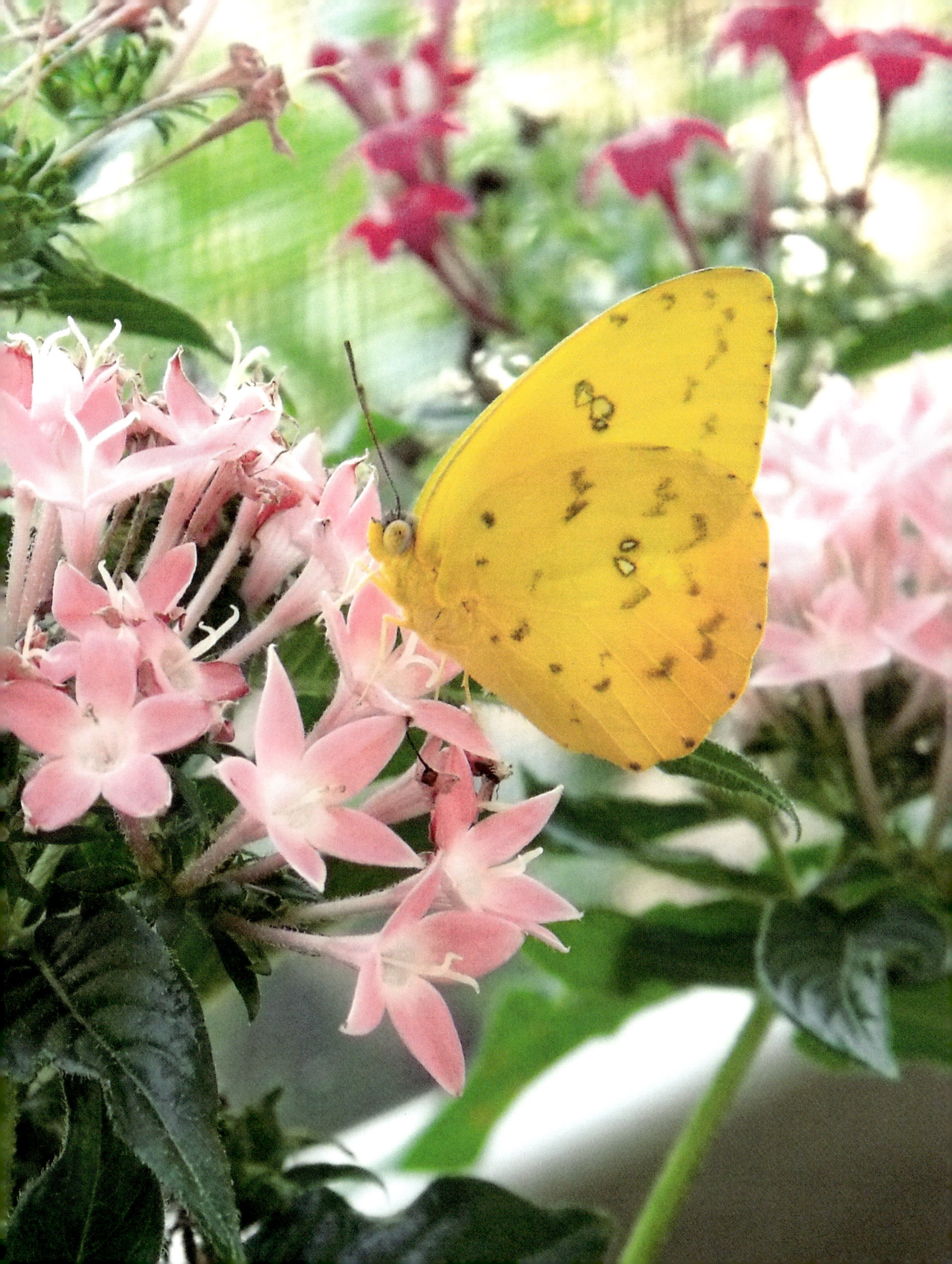

If You Plant It, They Will Come

They Just Disappeared!

One reason I started raising my own plants is because one day, I had no more potted plants to move indoors. I had close to thirty Monarch caterpillars and nothing inside to feed them. Since I had lots of plants planted around the house, I decided to move the caterpillars outside. I had no idea what a mistake that was. I went to check on them only ten minutes later and they were all gone. Something must have had a feeding frenzy! I didn't even think about it being a problem because I had read how they are poisonous when eaten, but something got them and made short work of it too. So, lesson learned. Now, I will even resort to digging up a plant to bring inside when I run short. I also learned that I can't rescue all of them. Sometimes, you just have to let nature take its course. With butterflies laying up to 300 eggs each, I just would not be able to support all of them. Now, I try not to over extend myself and just go by the number of plants I have. By rotating the caterpillars before they eat too much of the Milkweed, Pipevine or Cassia, I can keep the plants growing and feed a lot more caterpillars inside, where they are safe. Once they are large enough to leave their plant, I put them inside the Caterpillar Castle to start their transition to becoming a butterfly. This has worked well and allowed me to raise many more butterflies while keeping my plants growing. I have been doing this long enough to finally have the plant-to-caterpillar ratio working for me. Rarely do we have any more of these plant emergencies.

When needed, I can keep large plants in the breezeway.

Could this have been the culprit?

Where Did They Come From?

Although I work at it, I don't always catch the caterpillars before they become mature and start wandering off. Occasionally, I will see a caterpillar out for a stroll on the step and I put it in the Caterpillar Castle, but I don't always find them. As I stated earlier, I like to leave the caterpillars on plants in the breezeway because it is a more natural environment and I just think they do better there. Sometimes, they leave the plant and just vanish. That is one reason I keep track of the number of caterpillars I have. I may not be able to find them all, but at least, I know when they are missing. So, on days like today, it isn't really unusual to be surprised by new butterflies we didn't even know we had. That is a wonderful surprise and one we always welcome. I didn't see where these four Monarchs came from, but just this morning, we had three new males and one new female appear out of nowhere.

The front steps seem to be a nice place to hang out

Right around the corner, this guy emerged - could have easily been stepped on

These are artificial plants and the underside of these large leaves was a nice place for a chrysalis

Vince found a new friend in this little guy

If You Plant It, They Will Come

A rescued chrysalis

My first "patch" job, the butterfly was able to fly again

My 3rd attempt at repairing wings - This one was great!

The Doctor Is In

Sometimes, I will find a chrysalis on the ground and I have saved it by taping it to a pot, as shown in the first picture. I have also placed them on artificial plants. In all cases, the butterfly emerged without a problem. The picture in the middle is the first time I ever tried to repair a butterfly's wing. The patch was way too big and cumbersome, but it worked. The wing was badly bent and the butterfly couldn't fly. I actually watched a video on http://www.livemonarch.com about how to calm the butterfly so I could work on its wing. They can't fly when they get too cold, so I put the injured butterfly in a glass that had been in the freezer. In a short time, it calmed right down. I had some "crack and peel" that worked pretty well (except for being too large a piece.) Once the butterfly got used to the extra weight on its wing, it was able to fly away. I have greatly improved on my repair technique. The third picture shows a repair done with tape and glue. It was such a good job, this little lady chased away another butterfly and went on to lay a dozen or so eggs in the garden. I'm proud to say I've helped several butterflies that would have not been able to fly otherwise.

I've hung out my shingle and ... the Doctor is in!

The Spray Did Them In

Any time you live in a hot humid area, you probably have a mosquito problem. Last year, during the Summer months, I had no idea that planes flew over in the evening and sprayed for mosquitos. I was thankful for getting rid of those pests, but I didn't even realize that my caterpillars were insects too and would be affected by the spray. This was during my first year and after a spraying, I went out to find thirty of our caterpillars had died during the night. I was devastated! Vince called the Mosquito Abatement Center and discovered that they don't really have a set schedule for spraying. Usually, they test first and if there are mosquitos present, they spray. They did explain that they have a butterfly garden too and they test their spray to try and make sure it will not affect butterflies. Now, we have a much better arrangement because the Center told Vince they would put us on a "call list" to let us know when they were going to spray. We also talked to the gardeners that take care of neighboring homes and ask them to spray away from our house. Most of them know us now and are aware that we raise butterflies, so we have had fewer mishaps.

If You Plant It, They Will Come

Some Of My Neighbors Really Do Call Me
The Butterfly Whisperer

This picture and the previous one was taken on my Birthday and I was so delighted that these new butterflies chose this day
to emerge and wish me a Happy Birthday!

As I mentioned, butterflies can imprint on people and they do not shy away from them after that. It's really true. I have nursed a few back to health, mended wings and rescued them from predators. I just feel that butterflies are comfortable around me. I can pick them up, they land on me when I am working and I think they just sense that I am not going to hurt them. So, I can identify with Snow White, we both have little creatures that we call friends.

I Felt Like A Celebrity

I have to tell you, I was thrilled when our local Garden Club wanted to tour our little butterfly garden and sanctuary. I am always excited to talk about my caterpillars and butterflies, so we arranged a time for them to visit. When they arrived, I was a year and a half into the project and had already learned so much about these beautiful insects. The timing was perfect. I had eggs, caterpillars, chrysalises and butterflies to show them. They asked a lot of questions and I was happy that I could answer all of them. Although we only raise three different species, we had already released 293 butterflies and I still had almost fifty chrysalises left. This tour took place in November of last year and in the next newspaper, there was an article about me and my butterfly sanctuary.

I felt like a Rock Star when I would run into one of our neighbors and they would ask me if I was the "butterfly lady." I also give tours to the children and grandchildren of our friends and neighbors. The kids just love to hold the caterpillars (especially the boys.) I usually invite them over when the butterflies are ready to be released so they can participate. I even have a little carrying case so I can surprise a neighbor by releasing butterflies from their home. That is an unexpected treat and usually makes them smile.

Miraculous Migrating Monarchs

"We delight in the beauty of the butterfly, but rarely admit the changes it has gone through to achieve that beauty"

~Maya Angelou

If You Plant It, They Will Come

Monarchs hibernating in California Eucalyptus trees

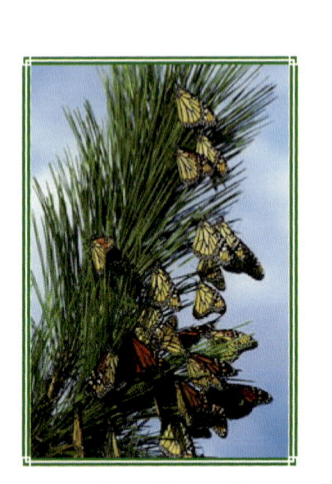

Monarchs will use the same trees year after year

You can't write a book about butterflies without mentioning how the Monarch migrates. Although that is usually the one fact people know about Monarchs, it is still such a mystery. No one really knows how the Monarchs find their way to or from their destination. So, I did some research on http://www.monarch-butterfly.com to make sure I had my facts straight. This is what I found: Monarch butterflies are not able to survive the cold winters of most of the United States so they migrate south and west each autumn to escape the cold weather. The Monarch migration usually starts in about October of each year, but can start earlier if the weather turns cold sooner than that. The Monarch butterflies will spend their winter hibernation in Mexico and some parts of Southern California where it is warm all year long. If the Monarch lives east of the Rocky Mountains, it will migrate to Mexico and hibernate in Oyamel fir trees.

Information source and photos by http://www.monarch-butterflies.com

It is quite a sight to see thousands upon thousands of these migrating Monarchs swarm to their final destination.

By hanging like shingles, they can stay warm

If the Monarch butterfly lives west of the Rocky Mountains, then it will hibernate in and around Pacific Grove, California in Eucalyptus trees. Wintering Monarchs cluster together. Each butterfly hangs with its wings over the butterfly beneath it, creating a shingle effect that buffers the butterflies from the rain and creates warmth. The weight of the cluster also prevents the butterflies from being blown away. Monarch butterflies use the very same trees each and every year when they migrate, which seems odd because they aren't the same butterflies that were there last year. These are the new fourth generation of Monarch butterflies, so how do they know which trees are the right ones to hibernate in? The amazing Monarch butterflies are the only insect that migrates to a warmer climate that is 2,500 miles away.

Information source http://www.monarch-butterflies.com

If You Plant It, They Will Come

I also watched a special on PBS about what a horrendous journey the Monarchs have; being battered with wind and rain as they fight their way south. The fourth generation can live up to nine months and make this journey in one trip, resting along the way. Of course, not all of them will complete the journey. Some may drown in the rain or get attacked by predators or just get so battered in the wind, their wings will no longer have the ability to keep them in the air. When you think about it, the Monarchs are really awesome. They have been tracked and monitored enough to know that they follow the same route year after year, but it is still not understood how they know which route to follow. Also, not every generation migrates, it is only the fourth generation that flies south each year. For the return trip, the butterfly mates, lays eggs, caterpillars emerge, form chrysalises and butterflies emerge to start the process again. They go through this same routine three times as they return to their starting point. All of this is taking place while heading north. Once they get back home, they mate one last time, lay eggs, caterpillars emerge, form chrysalises and it is only this fourth generation that will migrate south again.

This brings up an interesting point. The jury is still out on whether or not Florida Monarch butterflies migrate. We have Milkweed all year, the climate is warm all year and I see butterflies all year. Cold climate and lack of host plants are the main reasons for migration. Recently there was an article in The News-Press about how it is still a big mystery as to what Florida Monarchs do.

The North American Butterfly Association launched a butterfly tagging project last November because the Florida Monarch has never been researched. With Monarchs in Florida year-round, it is really difficult to know if they stay here and reproduce generation after generation or if they migrate to Mexico or California. They may even go north in the Spring, I really can't say. One gentleman said he had been casually observing and occasionally tagging his own butterflies for ten years and he still didn't have an answer. I can tell you one thing, our butterflies have flown off and come back to lay eggs. I know this because I have had a few that I had repaired their wings and I could identify them. On more than one occasion, they have flown right into the breezeway and I just don't think that is a coincidence. My opinion is that Florida Monarchs do not migrate. Although, just my opinion, it makes the most sense.

If You Plant It, They Will Come

Danger All Around Them

"The butterfly counts not months,
but moments, and yet has time enough."

~ Rabinhranath Tagore

If You Plant It, They Will Come

The butterfly really does have a tough life. It is a miracle that they ever come into being at all. I read that only 2% of the eggs ever make it to adulthood. I have seen butterflies actually chasing off bees so they could lay their eggs in peace. I have also seen wasps follow right behind butterflies and pick up the eggs. Once the caterpillar eats its way out of the egg, it could be attacked by ants, wasps, spiders, lizards or frogs. If they are lucky enough to get to the chrysalis stage, that isn't even a guarantee that they will become a butterfly. I really thought, once the chrysalis was formed, the butterfly would be safe, but a wasp will actually eat a chrysalis and so will ants. That's why I sealed the breezeway; I'm trying to keep all these predators out and keep our caterpillars and butterflies safe.

One day, I wasn't careful when I put a Cassia plant inside the Caterpillar Castle. I didn't notice that there were ants on the plant. I read that some ants actually protect the caterpillars, but these were carnivores. As soon as the chrysalis was formed, the ants swarmed it and killed the morphing caterpillar. I felt terrible because I had put the plant inside the safe haven and cost the butterfly its life. Devious little ants! They will actually hide under a leaf until you pass by. They also hide deep within the flower blossoms, making them easy to miss. They are perfectly still, so you may not notice them until you disturb the leaf itself, then they will scatter. Other than washing the plant with Dawn, I haven't found any way to completely eliminate ants.

I have yet to figure out which are "good" ants and which are "bad" ants. They all look alike to me, but some kill the caterpillars and some do not. I have read so much about ants and still have not figured out how to rid our plants of them. Maybe I shouldn't even worry about it, but the Senna/Cassia has special nodes that emits a sweet liquid. This attracts ants, bees and wasps. This is where I have seen the wasps follow right behind an Orange-barred Sulphur butterfly and pick up the eggs. I also saw ants swarming a tiny little caterpillar and killing it. So, I always thought ants were all bad, but I read other articles that talked about ants "milking" caterpillars for a sweet liquid secreted from their backs and these ants are said to protect the caterpillar from other predators. I have to admit, I've seen some ants walk over the Monarch and Gulf Fritillary caterpillars and the caterpillars don't seem to mind it. So, I think I am dealing with different kinds of ants. Some I have seen come out of the ground and others only seem to be on the plants themselves. I was told white vinegar will keep them at bay, so I tried it. It got rid of the ants, but the smell was so strong, I was afraid it would harm the butterflies, so I quickly washed it away. The next day, the ants were back. It is an on-going battle that we live with, but I'm starting to look at it as a natural part of the environment. I just work on keeping them out of the breezeway and away from the caterpillars. I just can't rid the entire garden outside of intruders, so I let Mother Nature balance that part out herself.

If You Plant It, They Will Come

Just when you think everything is running smoothly, some other problem arises. Our Milkweed was blooming, our butterflies were thriving, then I noticed these pests. You can see the Milkweed bugs in the picture with our beautiful Monarch! These black and orange insects have just about taken over our precious food source. I have yet to find an insecticide that will not kill the caterpillars and butterflies.

Consequently, I remove them by hand and this year they are particularly bad, so I spend a lot of time chasing bugs. They will lay hundreds of eggs, so you need to get rid of them. When you come across eggs or babies, you can spray them off with the hose, but I usually have to put on gloves and squash the adults to kill them. If you don't do that, your plants will start to suffer and pretty soon, no plants, no butterflies. It is a vicious cycle, but worth pursuing to keep the plants healthy.

The chrysalis on the next page is not just in the shade, it is actually black. You can see the healthy green chrysalis just below it. I know the chrysalis gets darker when the butterfly is about to emerge, but I could always see the outline of the wings before. This one was completely black. I searched the internet to find out what had happened. Sure enough, there is something called Black Death. I found some information on http://www.learnaboutmonarchs.com. Here is part of what I read. Black Death is usually caused by either a bacterial (Pseudomonas) or viral (Nuclear polyhedrosis) infection. Oh no, I didn't know I was going to have to become a nurse too! The caterpillar suddenly stops eating and there is an implosion, of sorts, that turns it a brownish-black color. This bacteria thrives in warm, moist environments. When I read that, I really paid attention because I have three incubators that I use to gather eggs and raise tiny caterpillars. Since I made them out of plastic containers, I really watch for moisture building up on the sides. They have a moist paper towel in the bottom to keep the leaves fresh and I do replace the leaves and the paper towels every day. I want to make sure I am not creating an environment that could cause mold to grow on the leaves and make the caterpillars sick. Also, the breezeway is not air conditioned and we are at the mercy of Mother Nature. If it gets too hot or too cold, I have been known to bring the caterpillars and butterflies indoors. A word of caution here: Keep an eye on the caterpillars, they have a tendency to stray.

Info Source - http://www.MonarchParasites.UGA.EDU/parasites & http://www.learnaboutmonarchs.com

If You Plant It, They Will Come

I just removed the chrysalis and cleaned the container, thank heavens, this was the only one I saw.

Releasing The Butterflies

"We are like the butterflies who flutter

for a day and think it's forever."

~Carl Sagan

If You Plant It, They Will Come

On this day, we had eleven butterflies ready to be set free. We invited our friends, Will and Rose Aubut to come share in the joy of releasing them. Will is on the lower right. He made a friend of one of the Swallowtails before letting it go.

Rose took the pictures of us releasing the rest.

Photos by Rose Aubut

112

If You Plant It, They Will Come

Just waiting to be released

Some choose to hang out in the yard

Others stop for lunch before they leave

We don't keep the butterflies around for long, so people have asked me why we go through the trouble. Butterflies are beautiful and if we can do something to add more beauty to this world, why not? I have always been the kind of person that just wants to take things one step further. When I started walking for my health, I wanted to push myself to start running and then enter races. When I was in sales, I wanted to be in the top ten percent. When I was a leasing agent, I wanted to become the leasing agent of the year and then the manager. Even when I worked as a park ranger, I wanted to become the lead ranger. I was able to accomplish all those goals, so I guess it is an inherent part of my being. I wasn't satisfied with a butterfly garden; I had to take the next step and raise my own butterflies.

When you look at our whole setup, it may look like a lot of work, but I hardly notice because I really enjoy every aspect of it. My Dad always said "Any time you can do something to increase your knowledge, that is a thing worth doing."

I have learned a tremendous amount by doing this project. I now have a dream to own a little piece of land large enough to build a greenhouse and butterfly conservatory. That may never happen, but everyone should have a dream. I still have no desire to do it for profit, I just like the pure enjoyment and beauty of it.

A Few Things I Learned Along The Way

Butterflies are self-propelled flowers.

~R.H. Heinlein

Because I had done this myself, I found this story very interesting.

One day a man came upon a chrysalis of a butterfly. He saw the butterfly struggling to force its body through a small opening in the chrysalis. After several hours it seemed that the butterfly stopped making any progress. It appeared as if it had gotten as far as it could and it could not go any further. To be helpful, the man took a pair of scissors and snipped off the remaining bit of the chrysalis. The butterfly then emerge easily. But, it had a swollen body and small, shriveled wings. The man continued to watch the butterfly because he expected that, at any moment, the wings would enlarge and expand to be able to support the body, which would contract in time. Neither happened! In fact, the butterfly spent the rest of its life crawling around with a swollen body and shriveled wings. It never was able to fly. The man in his kindness and haste did not understand – The struggle for the butterfly to go through the tiny opening in the restricting chrysalis is nature's way of forcing fluid from the body of the butterfly into its wings. This is a necessary process if the butterfly is to fly. So, the moral is, "Let nature take it's course and what will be is meant to be." (*author unknown*)

When I see butterflies struggling, I always want to help them too. After reading this story, I no longer help them out of their chrysalis! The one that I helped remained like the butterfly in the middle picture. The wings never fully developed. Every once in awhile, a butterfly will actually just die because it can't release itself from the chrysalis, but I just have to say, "It was meant to be" and let it go at that.

Monarch just starting to emerge

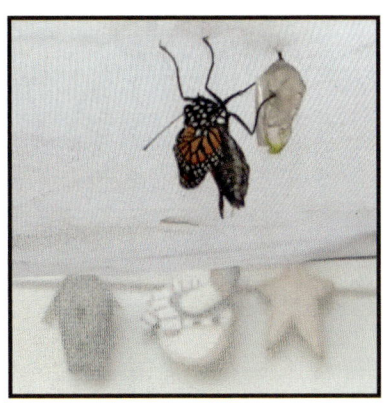

Newly emerged Monarch - note the large abdomen

The wings will unfurl when left undisturbed

Here are a few other things I learned about raising butterflies..........

1. The eggs will hatch in about 4-5 days. The emerging caterpillar is so tiny, it is hard to see until it is about three days old. Then, it is still tiny, but al least you can see it. The very first day, it just looks like a black speck on the leaf, but once I became accustomed to looking for them, I could spot them right away.

2. The butterfly lays its eggs on the "host" plant which is the food-source for the larva or caterpillar. This means the plant is going to be eaten, so if you don't want your garden to be destroyed, you need to remove the caterpillar and either place it on a plant reserved for eating, or cut a leaf of the plant with the caterpillar/egg on it and keep it in a container or jar.

3. Caterpillars eat A LOT! That is why I grow my own plants and keep them in pots. This allows me to rotate the growing caterpillars from one plant to another, giving them a fresh supply of food and giving the old plant a chance to re-grow and get ready for the next time it is needed. Just to give you an example; I had 20 Monarch caterpillars and I went through thirteen medium-sized plants before they started the chrysalis stage. The tiny babies don't eat too much, but the closer they get to the forming of a chrysalis, the more they eat and the more they eliminate waste. Before I got the Caterpillar Castles, I was sweeping up the breezeway twice a day.

4. A caterpillar will only eat its host plant, so if you want to raise different types of butterflies, you will have to have several different host plants. For example - The host plant for the Polydamas and the Pipevine Swallowtail is the Dutchman's Pipevine. Although there are four other types of Swallowtails in this area, they all have different host plants. Here are the host plants for each; Black Swallowtail - Dill and Fennel, Zebra Swallowtail - Pawpaws, Eastern Tiger Swallowtail - Sweet Bay and Wild Cherry and Giant Swallowtail - Wild Lime and Citrus plants.

Sometimes, you get lucky and several butterflies will use the same host plant. The Soldier, Monarch and Queen all use the Milkweed or Butterfly Weed as a host plant. The Zebra Longwing, the Julia and the Gulf Fritillary all use the Corky-stemmed Passion Vine or the Purple Passionflower for their host plant. So, you can see, unless you have a large yard and a lot to invest in plants, it is necessary to decide which butterflies you are most interested in raising or supporting. You can also grow your own plants to increase the volume.

5. A caterpillar grows so quickly, it will shed it's skin four or five times before it becomes a butterfly. I have heard various numbers of shedding times and I didn't observe one caterpillar shedding more than twice myself, so that is why I don't know the exact number. I can only tell you, from the number of skins I cleaned up, it is multiple times per caterpillar. It took me a little while to realize that my caterpillars were shedding, not dying. When they form the chrysalis, that is considered their final shedding. I was always happy when they got to that stage because they stopped eating!

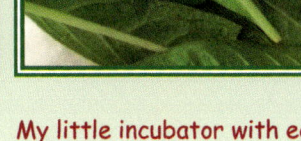

Three day old Monarch caterpillar

My little incubator with eggs and tiny caterpillars

Monarch caterpillar leaving the discarded skin it just shed

6. The Swallowtail butterflies are more sensitive to the changing seasons than our other butterflies. We had a few cold days that seemed to send the Swallowtails into a "hibernation" state. When it is warm, they emerge from their chrysalis in ten to fourteen days. However, our last batch didn't come out for five months. I guess they are more used to a "butterfly season" that usually runs from April to October.

7. I am certainly no expert on butterflies because I think the Viceroy and Monarch look alike. The Soldier and Queen are very close, as well as the Gulf Fritillary and the Julia Heliconia. I still have a hard time distinguishing the Orange-barred Sulphur from the Cloudless Sulphur. If I don't see orange, I'm just guessing.

8. The Swallowtails and Monarchs are poisonous to their predators (but not to humans) because of their host plants. That is why, birds tend to leave them alone. I actually saw a gecko pick up a Swallowtail caterpillar and spit it out. Unfortunately, the caterpillar still died, but that gecko learned not to try to eat any more caterpillars.

9. I noticed that some of our butterflies, chrysalises and caterpillars were larger than others, so I did some research to get some answers and found this information: "The size of the adult butterfly is determined by the size of the chrysalis and the larger the caterpillar, the larger the chrysalis. The more a caterpillar eats, the larger it will grow. If the caterpillar has to travel to look for another host plant after it has eaten the first plant, energy from its meal will be used to travel instead of being used to grow larger."

Well, that made sense to me, so I supply as much food as possible. Sometimes, I would be away for the day and upon my return, would find the host plant had been totally eaten and the caterpillars were just wandering around. As soon as I put a new host plant inside the Caterpillar Castle, the caterpillars would climb on and start eating again.

If You Plant It, They Will Come

The butterflies don't seem to mind being handled. Some even act like they just don't want to leave. We don't force them to go. If they will eat, we will keep them until they are ready to go out on their own.

119

Another reason for the difference in size is simply whether the butterfly is a male or female. In some species, like the Monarch, the male butterflies tend to be a little larger than the females.

10. In the wild, a Monarch usually lays only one egg per plant, but in captivity, she can lay dozens on one plant. The egg is likely to be on the under-side of the leaf, but I have found them hidden in the buds and even on top of leaves. I've also seen two eggs next to each other, so I don't know if one or two butterflies were responsible for those eggs.

11. Butterflies are the adult, they do not grow. The caterpillar is the baby butterfly. Since I had seen smaller and larger Monarchs, Sulphurs and Swallowtails, I assumed that those were the babies...... you know what they say about assuming!

12. The female is ready to mate as soon as she emerges from the chrysalis and our butterflies seem to mate as soon as we released them. That's another reason we don't keep them in captivity very long and it is good for us because they start laying eggs and we can start a new generation right away.

13. Butterflies like sunny areas that are sheltered from the wind, but I have seen them hang on for dear life when the wind is blowing and even lay eggs while swaying in the breeze. Their feet are like velcro, so they have quite a grip. They don't fly on cool, overcast days because they cannot fly if their body temperature is less than 80 - 86 degrees. I read a few different numbers, but low to mid-eighties seems to be the consensus. I also know from my observation, that it is true. They really can't fly at all when it is cold.

14. When a butterfly's feet come in contact with a sweet liquid, its feeding straw unfolds. I saw this happen when I would place them on watermelon. Sometimes, I would still have some juice under my fingernail and the proboscis (feeding straw) would search across my fingers and go directly to the juice.

15. Someone asked me what butterflies are good for. Are you kidding me? They are such a thing of beauty, why do they have to be good for anything else? But, they are actually better pollinators than bees because they cover a wider territory. Bees tend to be more localized.

16. Caterpillars can live in harmony with each other, but it is still survival of the fittest (so to speak.) On the same plant, some caterpillars get very large while others will remain small. Let's face it, some of them are pigs. The big guys do push the little ones around so they can eat more. I started taking the little, younger caterpillars out of the mix to give them a better chance at growing bigger. Once they get to a healthy size, they can fend for themselves, but the little ones will actually form a chrysalis when they really are too small. It is usually because some big guy has eaten all the food. I would rather have bigger butterflies, so I watch out for the little guys.

17. When you have nectar plants, you also have lots of bees, wasps, bugs and ants. Since it goes with the territory, I try to leave the environment as natural as possible. I don't want to spray anything that might harm the butterflies and caterpillars because they are insects too. So, that leaves out most sprays. If the pests get too bad, I either spray them with a jet of water, pick them off by hand or use a little soapy water. You just have to rinse the plants really well after the soap to get it all off the plant, otherwise the leaves will get burned by the sun.

18. I know butterflies really are able to identify a "home site" or an individual. I know this because too many of ours keep coming back. They also fly in and out of the breezeway when I leave the door open. I just don't think that is a coincidence.

19. Wonder where butterflies go when it rains? I found a whole group of our Swallowtails; hanging like leaves under the branches of our Dutchman's Pipevine.

Other Fun Facts:

Butterfly wings get their color from tiny scales. Their wings have 125,000 scales per square inch. Compare that to a human head, which has only about 100 hairs per square inch.

Most butterflies live 20 to 40 days. However, some species live only 3 or 4 days, while a few survive up to 10 months.

Butterfly wings often are brightly colored on top to attract mates or warn predators to stay away. The wing bottoms may be drab for camouflage.

Butterflies range in size from a tiny 1/8 inch to a huge almost 12 inches.

Butterflies and insects have their skeletons on the outside of their bodies, called the exoskeleton. This protects the insect and keeps water inside their bodies so they don't dry out.

Butterfly wings are actually transparent. The iridescent scales, which overlap like shingles on a roof, give the wings the colors that we see.

Contrary to popular belief, many butterflies can be held gently by the wings without harming the butterfly. Of course, some are more fragile than others, and are easily damaged if not handled very gently.

Both butterflies and moths belong to the order Lepidoptera. In Greek, this means scale wing.

Butterflies can see several colors as well as UV light.

The top butterfly flight speed is around 12 miles per hour. However, some moths can fly at speeds of up to 25 miles per hour.

Many butterflies can taste with their feet to find leaves to lay eggs on that are good for their caterpillars' food.

Information found at http://www.thebutterflysite.com and http://www.thebutterflypages.com

Strangers In The Midst

Sometimes you get things you don't even recognize. When I saw this first monster on my plants, I shrieked because it blended so well with the actual plant and I almost touched it. It looked like it would bite! I had no idea where it came from or what it was. At first I thought it was the caterpillar of a Lunar Moth, but when I found one on the internet, I realized it was a Tomato Horn Worm. We did have a few tomato plants in the breezeway and it must have come from one of those. No matter what it was, I didn't want it in our breezeway, It looked like it would eat everything in sight, so we removed it. I hate killing any creature, so I just put it outside and it wandered off to who knows where. A good place for all weird creatures, in my opinion.

I just threw these pictures in because I thought they were really strange looking moths. I had never seen anything like them, until we started raising butterflies. I thought they were interesting for two reasons; they were outside the breezeway and they both looked like they were made out of wood. The middle one had an intricate design on its wings and body and the last one looked like its wings were carved out of balsa wood.

Don't those teeth look like they could bite? This guy was huge!

This moth really was unique. I had never seen such an intricate design.

I wanted to put furniture polish on this one. It really looks like wood.

If You Plant It, They Will Come

2012

"Nature's message was always there
for us to see.
It was written on the wings of butterflies."

~Kjell B. Sandved

2012 brought some changes for us. The first thing I noticed is that we have only seen a few Swallowtail butterflies. I had three chrysalises left from last year; one emerged in February and the last two emerged in March. Besides those, I have only seen one or two others. By this time last year, we had released a total of 72 butterflies. Of those; 27 were Swallowtails, 30 were Monarchs and 15 were Sulphurs. The year is almost half over and I have had no Swallowtail eggs or caterpillars. We have released 80 butterflies so far this year, but only 8 of them were Sulphurs and the rest were Monarchs.

The Monarchs really seem to be thriving and that allowed me to experiment with trying to get them to mate in captivity. I have read so much about studies being done to determine how often Monarchs mate and how many eggs they lay and how many mates they have. All of this was being done in captivity, so I wanted to give it another shot and see if I could get a pair to mate. My problem in the past had been that I was afraid to keep them in captivity too long. Sometimes they wouldn't eat and it looked like they were getting weaker, so I would let them go, but we have a large area with lots of flowers and it seems reasonable that we should be able to keep them in captivity longer than we did last year. We still have the problem of them wanting to hang on the screen, but this year, I kept putting them on the plants and eventually, they started eating on their own. Once that happened, I wasn't afraid to keep them in captivity because I knew they would get nourishment. So, I had two males and two females that I decided to keep in the breezeway for as long as it took for them to mate. I read stories about males trying to mate before the females even got all the way out of the chrysalis, but mine didn't even seem to be interested in each other. I kept putting them on the Milkweed plant and noticed, after a day, they would stay there longer and longer. Just yesterday, I noticed them doing a little "mating dance" and I suspect that, at some point, they did mate. Within three days, I found a male Monarch with a broken wing and I'm guessing that he fell to the ground while mating. I'm not sure, but it seemed reasonable. Anyway, I patched up his wing and released him along with the other three. He flew off to live another day.

If You Plant It, They Will Come

I did find eggs on an indoor Milkweed, so our experiment was a success. However, I don't really see any reason to keep the butterflies captive longer than necessary. I really am fine with releasing them and collecting the eggs from the garden. I was just hoping that I could keep the butterflies around a little longer. The longer they stay in captivity, the easier it is for them to injure their wings because they don't understand the screen and they keep running into it or flapping their wings against it until they break. So, I'm going to stick to my original plan and keep releasing them as soon as they are strong enough to fly. We always have quite a few butterflies hanging around outside, to lay eggs. So, it really isn't necessary to keep them inside the screened area.

I played "Matchmaker" with these two hoping they would mate - and they did!

On the surface, you would think an incubator would be simple, but they require daily care. When the caterpillar emerges from its egg, you need to have fresh leaves available for the new babies. Since the paper towel is damp, I change it daily as well. Of course, the larger the caterpillars get, the more waste they eliminate and that is another reason for daily cleaning.

The new caterpillars are so minuscule, it is easy to "throw out the baby with the bath water," so keep an eye out for tiny little beings on the paper towel too. The Sulphur caterpillar really is the most difficult to see because it looks like a tiny leaf sprout. Before I discard anything, I frequently scour the incubator with a magnifying glass to make sure I haven't missed a tiny caterpillar.

I keep the caterpillars in the incubator until they are six or seven days old. By this time, I feel pretty secure about putting them on a plant in the breezeway. They stay on that plant until they start wandering, looking for a place to make a chrysalis. This is the point where I find a smaller plant to put inside the Caterpillar Castle, just in case they have a few more days of eating before they form a chrysalis. There is always an artificial plant in the container because several of them prefer that rather than building on their host plant or the container itself. This is where they will stay until they become butterflies.

If You Plant It, They Will Come

Three Different Incubators; Monarchs, Gulf Fritillary and Sulphurs

This year, I started collecting eggs and making incubators. They have been very successful and as a result, I already have more butterflies than we had last year.

New Pictures for 2012

If You Plant It, They Will Come

We have had a continual flow of Monarchs and we release them four and five at a time.

I have been rescuing more Sulphur eggs and the butterflies are plentiful.

My favorite pictures are the ones of the two different species sharing a plant and the Monarchs - I call that one "The four Amigos."

Gulf Fritillary

"Just living is not enough," said the butterfly,
"One must have sunshine, freedom, and
a little flower."

~Hans Christian Anderson

With 2012 also came the desire to expand our little universe of butterflies. We are adding a trellis archway to our Dutchman's Pipevine alcove in hopes of attracting that elusive Pipevine Swallowtail.

We also planted two Purple Passionflowers (shown above) and three Corky-stemmed Passion Vines to attract the Zebra Longwing. Once again, we didn't get the butterfly we were looking for. Once we bought the plants, we found that both these plants are also the host plant for the Julia and Gulf Fritillary.

So far, I have eggs, caterpillars and one chrysalis for the Gulf Fritillary. The eggs were tiny and looked like they could be the egg of the Zebra Longwing, but when the caterpillar appeared it was not the one I was hoping for. Although the caterpillar was not what I expected, the Gulf Fritillary is a beautiful little butterfly and one I am proud to add to our growing family. So, you just never know what fate has in store for you. I had never even seen a Gulf Fritillary and now we have released more than a dozen of them.

If You Plant It, They Will Come

Two tiny new eggs. We didn't know it at first, but these are Gulf Fritillary butterfly eggs

First Gulf Fritillary caterpillars. Orange with black hair - how cute!

Almost all the eggs I found were at the very end of the long stems, but I also found a few on the larger leaves. I had seen a few Gulf Fritillaries in the neighborhood, but had no idea what they were until I found these eggs and investigated on the internet. Now they are in the yard almost every day. Once you raise a few butterflies, you see that the stages are very much the same. These eggs produced caterpillars in five days and the caterpillar first ate its egg, then started to work on the plant leaf.

Although still tiny, these babies really looked twice the size of the Monarch babies. Since I didn't know anything about this species, I kept a close watch on them. When they shed their skin, it looks like a little ball of spikes because all you see is the hair sticking up. I was surprised to see a chrysalis on the host plant within twelve days. At first, I thought they were going to always stay on their host to form a chrysalis, but a few days later, some started to wander to the artificial plant as well.

If You Plant It, They Will Come

Up close, these caterpillars almost look wet. The orange is very shiny and the black hairs stick up like bristles on a brush.

Although aloof, they do look like they communicate. They also seem to get along with each other, no pushing or nudging - just a nod as they passed by.

133

If You Plant It, They Will Come

The head of this Gulf Fritillary caterpillar really resembles the head of an ant and maybe that is why the ants don't seem to bother them. Out in the garden, there were lots of ants on this Corky-Stemmed Passion Vine, but they actually crawled over the caterpillars and neither seemed to mind.

If You Plant It, They Will Come

The Gulf Fritillary does hang in the "J" position, similar to the Monarch, and its chrysalis is very similar to the Swallowtail. In this picture, there are two Gulf Fritillary caterpillars getting ready to become a chrysalis, a green Monarch chrysalis on the left, and under the red leaf, there is a little wad of bristles. That is the skin that was shed from one of the caterpillars. The third Gulf Fritillary (top center) is still looking for a spot to rest and on the far right is a Gulf Fritillary chrysalis.

If You Plant It, They Will Come

Gulf Fritillary Chrysalis

Polydamas Swallowtail Chrysalis

The Gulf Fritillary chrysalis looks similar to the Swallowtail chrysalis, but much smaller and it is hanging upside down and backwards. This one really looks like a dried leaf and seems to be attached by only one end.

I always thought the chrysalis for the Polydamas Swallowtail looked like a little seahorse. It does have very distinctive ears and a nose. You can barely see the little threads holding the chrysalis to the plant, but they are strong. Even after the butterfly emerges, I have to cut the chrysalis down because it is still holding firmly to the branch.

Within minutes after being formed, the Gulf Fritillary chrysalis really started looking more shrunken and dried out. It closely resembles a dried, dead leaf and I guess that is part of their protection. Even their host plant seemed to look dead and I probably would have gotten rid of it, but I found some eggs on the dried tendrils. Thank heavens, I kept the plant because, although it looked like it was totally dead, it started sprouting green leaves again. I think there must be some kind of growing cycle they go through because my two other plants looked like they were about dead when, just like the Phoenix, they rose from the ashes. So, don't be too quick to toss a seemingly dead plant; It just might surprise you.

The chrysalis actually dried and twisted after it was formed. The clear shells are empty Monarch chrysalises.

If You Plant It, They Will Come

Our very first Gulf Fritillary

What a beautiful little butterfly!

Almost two butterflies in one

Already waiting to leave the nest

This is the underside of the wing and it looks like a completely different butterfly. The markings are very distinctive. It looks white in the picture, but the markings are actually a beautiful shimmering silver color.

This little butterfly is 2.75 inches, but compared to the Monarchs, it looks very tiny. They seem to do everything faster, they were out of the chrysalis and ready to fly within minutes, so we didn't keep them inside the breezeway for more than an afternoon.

Zebra Longwing

Love is like a butterfly, it goes where it pleases and it pleases wherever it goes.

~Author Unknown

If You Plant It, They Will Come

This picture was taken at The Butterfly Estates

The Zebra Longwing was one of the most abundant butterflies in the garden. Vince was able to get several really nice pictures and the butterflies didn't mind posing for us.

A beautiful pair of Zebra Longwings

Although we have seen many of these in our neighborhood, we have yet to entice a female to lay her eggs in our garden. The host plant is Purple Passionflower and we planted some just this year. A female may produce several generations each year, so we have a chance to gather some eggs of our own. It's like an Easter egg hunt. We are still looking for those elusive eggs.

If You Plant It, They Will Come

Chrysalis of the Zebra Longwing, very similar to the Gulf Fritillary

The caterpillar (pictured above) for this beautiful butterfly is also as unique as the butterfly itself.

These pictures were all taken by Vince at The Butterfly Estates in Fort Myers, Florida

If You Plant It, They Will Come

The Zebra Longwing was designated as the Florida state butterfly in 1996. It is found throughout the state, but most common in South Florida.

When I first saw these Zebra Longwings at the Butterfly Estates, I was very surprised because I thought they looked a lot bigger flying in the outdoors. I read the information about them and it said their wingspan is 3 to 3.25 inches. That really is a pretty standard size for a butterfly. It also said they can live from two to six months and that is much longer than most butterflies live. As far as I know, the only other butterfly with that long a life span is the fourth generation Migrating Monarch. The Zebra Longwing is the only butterfly known to eat nectar and pollen. All other butterflies only eat nectar.

If you are fortunate enough to see one, they are very beautiful as they glide through the air. This year, we planted some Corky-stemmed Passion Vine and some Purple Passionflower (the host plant) in an attempt to lure them into our yard. I have seen several in the neighborhood and I would love to have some eggs to start a family of our own. I have gotten several eggs already, but they have all been from the Gulf Fritillary which also uses the same host plant.

If You Plant It, They Will Come

Butterfly Estates

Butterflies...flowers that fly and all but sing

~Robert Frost

If You Plant It, They Will Come

If You Plant It, They Will Come

The Butterfly Estates is located at 1815 Fowler Street, Fort Myers, Florida. It's three thousand six hundred and fourteen square foot Glazed Glass Butterfly Conservatory houses 400 to 1500 free-flying butterflies that delight guests with their astounding color variations. The fully automated glass structure was commissioned by the project owners in 2006 to create the best possible environment for the sole purpose of protecting and conserving Florida Native Butterfly Species.

One thing I loved about The Butterfly Estates is the fact that you can stay as long as you want. We called to find out the best time to go and went on a day when they usually didn't get a lot of traffic. We wanted to be able to take our time and take pictures while we were there. If we had the room, I would love our little sanctuary to look just like this. While there, I felt so at peace with nature. The little benches scattered about created a tranquil place to sit and just observe. If you are lucky, one of the butterflies might even land on you, especially if they like your scent or a color your are wearing.

*Information source - http://www.thebutterflyestates.com

If You Plant It, They Will Come

If You Plant It, They Will Come

My Butterfly Notes and Observations

Just like the butterfly, I too will awaken in my own time.

~ Deborah Chaskin

June 29, 2010
Today we prepared the soil to get ready for the beginning of our butterfly garden. We found a nursery that had Dutchman's Pipevine plants! We bought pots, soil, and a few trellises, we are ready to go - how exciting is this?

July 8, 2010
We wanted to start with Swallowtails and we were lucky enough to find two plants that already had 5 caterpillars on them at the nursery. Out of the 5 caterpillars two died, one went MIA and two are in chrysalises. Two would be fine to produce butterflies and lay new eggs, but we don't know if they are male or female or both the same sex.

July 17, 2010
Now that our Pipevine plants are doing well, we may not have any Swallowtails to lay eggs on them. This has turned into a real project. Our breezeway, looks really nice though. We have trellises covered with beautiful Pipevine plants and lots of planters filled with nectar flowers. We also have plants outside in the yard to try to lure any visitors that may decide to lay eggs. It is a fun, beautiful project and if we can get the Swallowtails going, we will have improved the population of a rare Florida butterfly. I am like an expectant mother, checking my babies every day watching for signs of emerging butterflies. We should have a family soon and I can't wait.

August 8, 2010
We quickly added Monarchs to our family and there are always Monarchs laying eggs on the Milkweed plants that are out in yard. They start out so small, but the caterpillars seemed to grow every time I looked at them. It wasn't long before we had chrysalises hanging all over the place.

August 10, 2010
Our first Swallowtail arrived today! Although the eggs were laid on our Dutchman's Pipevine, this butterfly isn't a Pipevine Swallowtail, it is called a Polydamas Swallowtail. I called it a Pipevine Swallowtail for months before I was corrected. I don't care what it's called, it is beautiful.

August 19, 2010
Ten Monarchs came out of their chrysalises today. That is the most I have ever had appear in one day. I am PLEASED!!!!

August 21, 2010

Today was a sad, happy day for me. We released ten new Monarch butterflies into the wild and I was sad to see them go. They just made me smile every time I looked at them, but we couldn't keep them caged in, they just wanted to fly. So, today was the day I said good-bye. Now I have "empty nest syndrome."

September 16, 2010

We are almost three months into developing a butterfly garden and enclosed sanctuary. We started out doing great and had released about 28 butterflies when our neighbor sprayed with pesticides for the first time. There is a fair amount of distance between our houses, but within hours, our Monarch caterpillars started dying. The ones that didn't die had problems forming a chrysalis and sometimes only got partially developed before they died. The ones that had successfully formed a chrysalis produced butterflies with wings so misshapen, they couldn't fly and ended up dying within two days. We had 30 Sulphur caterpillars that all died within a day. We had been growing plants especially for the specific type of butterfly and rotating them as the caterpillars ate the plants. You can imagine our devastation when our hard work started going down the drain. The spray didn't seem to affect the Swallowtails, perhaps because they are stronger. Swallowtails and their host plant (the Dutchman's Pipevine) are actually poisonous when eaten, but so are the Monarchs and their host, the Milkweed. After being wiped out, we washed down all the plants and set them outside. Before long, we had Monarchs and Sulphur butterflies laying eggs again.

October 12, 2010

Something is attacking my plants! It turned out to be mealy bugs. Fortunately we caught them in time and they were only on the Hibiscus. I did have to spray to get rid of them, but I have a lot of other plants, so the butterflies will still have plenty of nectar.

November 03, 2010

I have learned so much just by observing the butterflies and caterpillars. I have a "viewing cage" that is better than watching TV. For instance, the Swallowtails lay their eggs in clumps of 12 to 30 eggs. When those eggs hatch, that group of tiny babies usually stick together until they become much larger caterpillars. They eat and sleep together and form a line when they move from place to place.

November 14, 2010

I read about a butterfly season that ends in October, but I just had 35 Swallowtail eggs hatch and all tiny babies seem to be doing fine. The one thing I did notice is that the chrysalises are taking longer to open. In the north, where there are colder winters, they don't open until Spring and since our nights are getting a little colder, I may not see any new butterflies for a while. This new batch of chrysalises have already been hanging two weeks longer than my previous ones, so I don't know what to expect. I will just watch and wait to see.

November 25, 2010

We continued to have butterflies well into November. It did seem like it was taking the butterflies longer to emerge from their chrysalis, but I still had new Monarch and Sulphur butterflies. The Swallowtails were the ones that I thought might not appear until Spring, but some of them even emerged, albeit a little later than usual.

December 11, 2010

It started happening gradually, but I wasn't seeing any more eggs on my plants. So, I still don't know if I will have to wait until Spring to see this new batch of butterflies. Since it doesn't usually get too cold here, I may have some Christmas butterflies. If not, we will have a whole group in the Spring! We have released 107 since we started and it has been a wonderful experience. Vince created a beautiful website for me to share my stories. http://www.cynthiasbutterflygarden.com

December 25, 2010 - Merry Christmas!

After a month of waiting, one Swallowtail emerged on Christmas Eve and one on Christmas Day. What a delightful surprise.

May 25, 2011

Since the first of 2011, we have released 107 Monarch, Swallowtail and Sulphur butterflies. January and February were really not very productive months, but I still have a lot of chrysalises and we still released ten butterflies a month for those first two months. March was a busier month and we released 19, but April and May were stellar months with a total of 67 butterflies being released in that 60 day period - Wow!

June 2, 2011
I had five Swallowtail caterpillars devour a full-size Pipevine plant in ten days and when you have to replace them, it gets pretty expensive. I finally got some to grow from seeds. I also had some luck with cuttings, but that has been kind of hit and miss.

June 5, 2011
I have found that Monarchs are really affectionate. I wonder if, because I handle them from the time they are caterpillars, they sense that I won't harm them. We recently had a batch of Monarchs that all had some kind of problem. This ranged from minor wrinkled wings to debilitating wings, that were not fully formed or wouldn't open. These are the little guys that I keep inside the breezeway because they usually can't fly. I feed them watermelon, honeydew melon and crushed apples in a water and sugar solution. As long as they eat, they can get stronger and sometimes overcome their disability. It does my heart good to see one of these babies fly away.

September 22, 2011
I watched a video on how to repair a butterfly's wing today. I don't know if I really want to try it though. I did rescue a caterpillar that I thought had drowned. I must have just caught it in time, because after I pulled it out of the water, it didn't take long for it to start crawling. I put it on a plant and it was fine.

January 01, 2012 - Happy New Year!
We released 447 butterflies in 2011. Not bad for a non-commercial, single family project.

February 26, 2012
Today (Dad's Birthday) is the day I made up my mind to write a book about my butterfly experiences. My friend Rose wrote a book that turned out beautifully. She inspired me to write one about something I know, so I started a book about butterflies.

March 3, 2012
I met my friend from SparkPeople today, Jennifer Knoll. What a wonderful person. We had no butterflies the day of her visit, but she enjoyed the caterpillars and contributed several pictures of Monarch caterpillars to my collection.

May 14, 2012
We bought two Purple Passionflowers and some Corkystem Passion Vine, in the hopes of attracting the Zebra Longwing. Since it is the Florida state butterfly, we would like to raise it. I have seen them in the neighborhood, so maybe we can get lucky.

May 17, 2012
This morning I found two eggs on our Purple Passionflower. I don't know for sure, but I think they may be Zebra Longwing. I brought them inside and put them in my little incubator. I should know within four or five days. If the caterpillar is white, we will have a winner!

May 21, 2012
The caterpillars emerged from their eggs this morning and they are not white. I think they are Gulf Fritillary. That is OK with me. I welcome them, whatever they are.

May 27, 2012
The caterpillars are growing quickly and we will soon have a chrysalis.

June 1, 2012 - Happy Birthday!
Today is my Birthday and five new Monarch butterflies chose this time to emerge and wish me a happy day. What a fantastic Birthday present!

June 3, 2012
My friend, Jennifer Knoll came to visit again and we had a wonderful surprise. Our very first Gulf Fritillary emerged today. What a beautiful butterfly. Jen brought her camera and took some wonderful pictures. Fortune was smiling upon us that day because she was also able to get some fantastic shots of Monarchs mating...Priceless!

June 19, 2012
We have now released twelve Gulf Fritillary butterflies and the work on my book is finished. Just a few minor corrections, but it is completed! I will start editing today.

June 21, 2012
The Polydamas Swallowtails are back! This morning, I checked my plants and found 12 newly emerged caterpillars. Boy, am I thrilled, I thought they were gone for good. So, I have added one new incubator to the collection and another page to my book.

If You Plant It, They Will Come

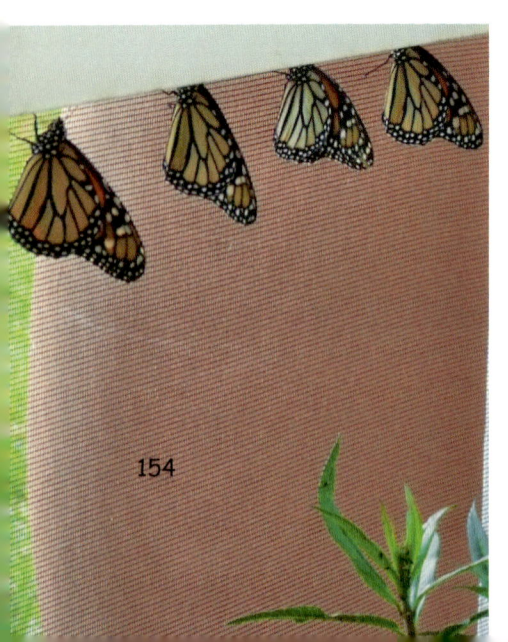

Acknowledgements

"What the caterpillar calls the end of the world,
the Master calls a butterfly.

~Richard Bach

If You Plant It, They Will Come

I used the internet to read about plants and butterflies and several times, I would find differing information. It got a little frustrating because some of the information was incorrect. Once I had eggs, butterflies and caterpillars, I started studying my own insects and jotted down what I had learned. Since I live in Florida, this information may vary a little for your area.

It was refreshing to find several places on the internet that gave factual information and I would like to acknowledge them as my other sources:

http://www.learnaboutmonarchs.com
http://www.livemonarch.com
http://www.butterflypages.com
http://www.Monarch-Butterfly.com
http://www.TheButterflySite.com
http://www.Butterflyfunfacts.com
http://www.MonarchParasites.uga.edu/parasites.com
http://www.The Butterfly Estates.com

I also want to thank these wonderful individuals for contributing to the beautiful pictures of our growing butterfly family.

Rosemary Aubut
Vince DeMattia (My Honey)
Julie (Harrington) Iven
Jennifer Knoll

A quote from my Dad - "If you can't do something right, don't do it at all."

I think we did this right!

If You Plant It, They Will Come

If You Plant It, They Will Come

For the past two and a half years, I raised butterflies for my own pleasure and kept a journal of the entire process from egg to adult. I observed the habits and personalities of both the caterpillars and the butterflies themselves.

You won't find many Latin words or scientific explanations in this book, but I hope it piques your interest enough to read it anyway.

The process was very educational, entertaining and sometimes, even heartbreaking. It is a story you might enjoy reading and perhaps be able to learn a few new things along the way.

Cynthia Harrington

Cynthia graduated from the University of San Francisco with a BS degree in Human Relations and Organizational Behavior and retired from AT&T after more than thirty years of service.

She and I traveled throughout the Southern United States in a 32' motor home which would be our only residence for over two years. We ended our adventure in Las Vegas, where we stayed for nearly five years before returning to Florida.

With more time on her hands, Cynthia planted flowers that attracted butterflies and began her quest to create a butterfly sanctuary. We currently raise four butterfly species; Monarch, Sulphur, Swallowtail and Gulf Fritillary. We are hoping for Zebra Longwings before we are finished so, ... the saga continues.

Vince DeMattia